T5-AST-993

TAKING BACK OUR CHILDREN

A Reader to Foster Dialogue around Youth Justice Reform

Criminology students from Queensborough Community College and formerly incarcerated writers come together at a campus reading meant to change hearts and minds.

TAKING BACK OUR CHILDREN

A Reader to Foster Dialogue around Youth Justice Reform

Correctional Association OF NEW YORK

First American edition published by Herstory Writers Workshop, Inc. 2013

Copyright © 2013 by Herstory Writers Workshop

Second printing 2013

All rights reserved
Manufactured in the United States of America

ISBN: 978-0-9893533-0-4

Front cover photos: Randee Daddona (*Newsday* Sept. 23, 2012) Liena Gurevich*
Frontispiece photo: Rose-Marie Aikas
Flower images photographed by Linda Coleman

The nine stories in "Young Voices from Jail" and "How Do You See Me?" by
Angelique Wadlington first appeared in *VOICES: Memoirs from Long Island's
Correctional Facilities*, published by Herstory Writers Workshop in 2012.

Herstory Writers Workshop, Inc.
2539 Middle Country Rd. FL 2
Centereach, New York 11720
Phone: 631-676-7395
Fax: 631-676-7396
www.herstorywriters.org

Newsday photo depicts correction officers Captain Helen Geslak, Lieutenant
Darleen McClurken and Sergeant Noreen Fisher in a sharing circle with Herstory
and community members.

Portrait is of Denise Irby, author of "The Birth" claiming her own story with her
picture attached to it in freedom.

Frontispiece photo shows criminology students at Queensborough Community
College and formerly incarcerated writers coming together at a campus reading
from *VOICES*.

Contents

Acknowledgements

When We Care Deeply Enough

When we care deeply enough, we find words we didn't know we had. Each of us has a "poetry of experience" hidden deep inside us that can be called into being out of the stream of memories that bubble up to the surface from our hope and our anger and grief. When we dare to imagine that someone might hear us and actually care, bit by bit, we break out of the silence and isolation that is the fate of so many.

But what is caring, really? It is so much more than a feeling passed along to another, going nowhere. It is—and must always be—a very deep call to action. Otherwise our belief in society's capacity to protect us will die even before it is properly born.

This folio edition of stories by adolescents writing from jail asks for a very specific kind of caring, about the fate of adolescents incarcerated before they have the chance to find paths away from the cycles of poverty, violence, addiction, abuse and despair into which so many were born.

It grows out of the work of Herstory Writers Workshop, an organization dedicated to using an empathy based technique of memoir writing to give a place in the discourse to those whose stories have been silenced and unsung, and is dedicated to the Raise the Age Campaign of the Juvenile Justice Project of the Correctional Association of New York, in a movement to raise the age at which juveniles are prosecuted and incarcerated as adults.

The stories in this collection were written over a two-year period by girls incarcerated in Long Island's three jails. They were generated in weekly workshops where the girls were helped to recreate moments out of their young journeys that would dare a reading stranger to care, without any emphasis on the nature of the actions that led to their incarceration of the actual experience of being in jail.

Thus, if we are to see these stories a call to action, it is in the largest sense that we must allow them to illuminate the systemic and societal realities in the lives of the young people our society incarcerates. As we look for alternative ways to break the cycles of early parental loss and addiction, poverty, discrimination, violence and abuse, we must sing these stories as those of heroes—not as pariahs to be silenced and locked away—realizing that most of us couldn't have been so brave in the face of the sort of adversity these young women describe.

After you finish reading, we invite you to turn to the back matter from the "Raise the Age" Campaign, to see how you might become involved, knowing that New York is one of only two states in the country—in company with North Carolina—that automatically prosecutes 16- and 17-year-olds as adults. New York also prosecutes 13-, 14- and 15-year-olds charged with certain serious offenses as adults.

These young people are subject to lifelong criminal records and drastic consequences including denial of educational loans, barriers to employment, deportation, and loss of housing for both themselves and their families. Children prosecuted as adults have been shown to return to prison at higher rates than those prosecuted in juvenile courts.

Whether you are reading this book in your prison cell or in a classroom, whether you are a corrections officer or someone just beginning to look at the impact of the criminal justice system, we hope that these stories will inspire you to add your own voice to whatever most needs to be said.

Erika Duncan
Founder and Artistic Director,
Herstory Writers Workshop
March, 2013

What Our Children Deserve

Our children deserve the very best that we can give them. They need to be nurtured, protected, guided and understood. If we fail to provide them with these important ingredients for healthy development and success, we guarantee their failure as adults. It takes a village to raise a child, and it takes a child to develop the best in the village.

What then, are we developing by locking our children away as adults? In fact, prosecuting children in adult courts and locking children up in adult jails and prisons increases crime. The myth that prosecuting children as adults reduces violence in our communities has been routinely debunked by volumes of research demonstrating that children prosecuted as adults actually recidivate at higher rates, and commit more acts of violence in the future than children prosecuted in the youth justice system. Prosecuting children as adults also harms children's ability to grow into healthy adulthood.

The youth justice system, while not perfect, provides children with more meaningful opportunities for rehabilitation. It is designed to serve young people, and thus is better than the adult system in meeting their educational, social and emotional needs. By contrast, children in adult courts and in adult jails and prisons are generally treated as if they are adults—an approach that fails both them and public safety. This is because the adult system provides children with little to no opportunity for developmentally appropriate services and rehabilitation, making it far less likely that youth will get the help they need to succeed.

New York, often a national leader in public policy, is woefully behind the rest of the country on this issue, remaining one of only two states to automatically treat all sixteen- and seventeen-year-olds in the justice system as adults. New York is also a national outlier in prosecuting some children as young as thirteen in adult courts. New York also confines 16- and 17-year-olds in adult jails and prisons.

It is extremely disturbing that New York State allows children in adult jails and prisons to be held in solitary confinement for days and months on end. While young people in solitary confinement may be separate from adults, they are by no means safe. Children in solitary confinement are locked in extremely small cells for up to twenty-three hours a day, with almost no contact with the external world. They are fed through a slot in the door, do not attend school, and their contact with other human beings is virtually non-existent. Prolonged solitary confinement is known to cause serious psychological and emotional trauma, including potentially irreparable harm. Children in solitary confinement fare even worse than adults, yet they frequently end up there.

Children in adult jails and prisons also face extremely high risks of sexual, emotional and physical abuse. For example, children in adult prisons are twice as likely to be beaten up by staff and far more likely to be attacked with a weapon as compared to young people in youth facilities. Children in adult jails are thirty-six times more likely to commit suicide than those in juvenile detention facilities.

In addition to enduring vast psychological and emotional trauma, children prosecuted as adults are often stigmatized for life. These children are subject to lifelong criminal records and drastic consequences including barriers to college admission, barriers to employment, potential loss of housing for them and their families, voting restrictions, and potential deportation. Countless doors forever shut behind these children based on actions they took before reaching high school graduation age.

Prosecuting children as adults contradicts everything we know about adolescence, including the fact that children's brains are still developing. We as a society recognize that children lack the sufficient cognitive and emotional maturity necessary to enter into cell phone contracts, go to a tanning booth, get married, purchase alcohol, vote, or get a tattoo. We require children to get parental consent before engaging in these activities or we ban them totally for children. Yet New York State allows those very same children to be questioned by the police without parental consent, housed in adult jails and prisons, and permanently stigmatized with criminal convictions.

The devastating impact of prosecuting children as adults is disproportionately born by children and communities of color. Nation-wide youth of color are arrested, charged and incarcerated more than white youth for similar conduct, though studies show they do not commit more crimes. New York State's justice system is marked by profound racial and ethnic disparities at every step in the process from arrest to incarceration rates.

Treating children in the justice system as children is not at odds with holding young people accountable for their behavior. The youth justice system simultaneously promotes accountability and provides opportunities for young people to receive the kinds of rigorous rehabilitative programs that are proven to work.

Beginning with laws passed in 1824 and the early 1900s, New York State has treated 16- and 17-year-olds in the justice system as adults. Over fifty years ago, as New York State's legislators created the Family Court, they discussed whether to raise the age at which young people could be tried as adults. Unable to reach consensus, the lawmakers of that era left the age of criminal responsibility at 16. A legislative committee emphasized that the decision was "tentative and subject to change" and urged further study, which did not happen. It is now past time to revisit that tragic decision. New York State must end the shameful practice of prosecuting children in adult courts and locking children up in adult jails and prisons. We cannot afford any more delay—the lives and well being of children and the safety of communities hang in the balance.

Soffiyah Elijah
Executive Director
The Correctional Association of New York

Angelo Pinto
Raise the Age *Campaign Manager*
The Correctional Association of New York

This photo is of Denise Irby, reading from "The Birth" (page 39) to criminology students at Hofstra University, as she holds the baby who was born during her incarceration, now proudly in freedom.

YOUNG VOICES
FROM JAIL

Introduction

Seventy thousand young people under the age of 18 woke up today behind bars in the United States. The vast majority of these young people are charged with non-violent crimes that posed no threat to public safety, but their futures will forever be complicated and marked by the effects of their arrests and incarceration. Most are youth of color and from low-income urban communities, whose offenses might well have been dismissed in more affluent white neighborhoods.[1] In spite of—or because of—their experiences behind bars, more than 70% of them will return to prison within a decade, often for more serious felonies, and to serve longer sentences.[2]

Almost all of the stories and faces of these young people—their boundless energy, their already guarded hopes and dreams that lurk beneath the stories of what brought them to brush with the criminal justice system—will never be known to us, but we are able to offer you a few of them here. It has been our great gift to see these hopes and dreams emerge bit by bit, as girls who had been rival gang members in the streets, looking for the love, community and power so absent from the almost unbearable burdens that marked their young lives, found a safe space to express how their choices were made.

What emerges from their stories is a poignant picture of the search for attachment, power over circumstances, and a means of survival that has motivated the choices of these young women so far. As they share their fantasies—that enough love might make the men to whom they have attached themselves not only kind but "bullet-proof," that the babies they bear while incarcerated will be theirs to raise differently, that perhaps women will be able to love differently from men, or that mothers enslaved to addiction might return to a beauty only vaguely remembered—we cannot help but want to put our arms around the young selves they have lovingly, angrily—even at times playfully—brought back to life on these pages.

Like the women you meet elsewhere in this anthology, the majority of these girls have already been marked by the system. They are children of mothers who were too wounded themselves to have anything left to give, foster children passed along as pawns in unsavory money-making schemes, and victims of generations of addiction, violence and abuse. As each takes on the task of connecting the dots, to show how she navigated life's circumstances, we gather more insight into what this dynamic tribe of incarcerated girls is up against, as we watch them struggle to find pleasure and mastery in the badly corrupted, broken places into which they have been thrown.

While for boys and men in many cultures, "doing time" can be seen as a rite of passage, women and girls who have brushed with the system are all too often shunned by the families and community members who celebrate this rite for their young men. We close this collection with the story of another kind of violence and violation, without which the picture would not be complete, paying tribute to the many children whose sense of safety and justice was violated irreparably during dangerous border crossings, while their parents struggled to find them a new life.

For, it is only in connecting the dots that we start to see the whole picture—the disproportionate number of young people of color who end up in jail, the relationship between domestic violence and larger violence, and the unequal distribution of resources and opportunities—each story contributing to the creation of a just, equitable world, where no one will need to undergo what these young women have undergone.

The teen writing that we have encountered in Suffolk and Nassau County's three jails, is steeped in the mores of their peers and the popular culture of Rap and HipHop. Often these young women begin their journey into memoir by writing in rhyme, a medium that allows them to both express and hide at the same time, and to speak to their peers in the language of their "tribe." Only slowly, over time do they garner the trust in their writing community that allows them to break free of the rhyming that shields them, and to enter the particulars of their life experience.

While in Nassau County Correctional Facility, incarcerated girls are separated from their elders in almost all of their activities, in Suffolk County's two facilities, freer mixing has allowed us to create workshop formats where the teens benefit by working alongside older women who serve as mentors and guides.

These are the "mothers" who may have cared for or abandoned them, whose stories they can hear and tears they can see, as they bear witness to their maternal pain, remorse, and regrets for their actions, as well as their concerns and worries for their own teen daughters in trouble. These women are living examples of issues they are struggling with in their own relationships with their own mothers (and for the many incarcerated teen mothers who appear in our groups.) Side by side they work, cry, and laugh together, nurturing forgiveness and acceptance.

Herstory was born out of the notion that caring on the part of a reading or listening stranger isn't unconditional, but must be carefully earned. For much as we, as "Stranger/Readers," try to be open-minded, we are intrinsically judgmental. What makes Herstory workshops unique—both inside jail-based settings and out—is our work with each writer to challenge the judgmental reader to enter so deeply that these barriers begin to dissolve. Never is this technique of daring the reader to care more important than in working with our incarcerated teens, who take judgment to its very limit. What they learn in the process of listening to the gradual opening of one another's stories, just as they are encouraged to go deeply into their own, is how their willingness to be vulnerable turns fear and judgment into empathy, creating a new sort of strength and community.

Although the young women included in this folio collection would have been thrilled to have their stories published under their own names, we have decided to create pseudonyms for those under the age of 18 still in custody of the state. As they come of age, in future editions or online publications, we will return those who remain in contact with us and continue with their justice work to their own identities and keep our readers up with what they have decided to do with their lives. For this reason too, we have decided to publish this collection with only flowers instead of the photographs so many of the young women had friends and relatives on the outside forward to us.

Linda Coleman and Erika Duncan
Summer 2012

Notes

1. As of 2010, over 83% of young people in locked facilities were African-American or Hispanic. While we are working specifically in jails, where arts organizations rarely go—writing workshops in prisons are more common—the figures we have given here, in order to give a broader overview, include teens in prison and post-trial facilities. Our teen program serves between 50 and 75 young women ages 16–21 incarcerated in Long Island's three jails, while our women's program serves well over 100 a year.

2. Thirty-eight states and the District of Columbia treat 17-year-olds as juveniles. Fewer than 10 states continue to treat 17-year-olds as adults. Illinois has recently amended its age of criminal responsibility to treat 17-year-olds who commit misdemeanors as juveniles. Connecticut raised its age of criminal responsibility to 17 effective January 2010. In 2012, Connecticut raised its age of criminal responsibility to 18. *(OJJDP Statistical Briefing Book.* Available: *http://ojjdp.nc-jrs.gov/ojstatbb/structure_process/qa04101.asp?qa Date=2007.* Released on October 31, 2009; Illinois Public Act 95-10310 effective January 1, 2010; Connecticut General Statutes section 46b-121.) By contrast, New York is one of only two states in the nation (the other is North Carolina) where all 16- and 17-year-olds in the justice system are automatically prosecuted as adults, without exception and regardless of crime severity. In a January 2011 report, *Advancing a Fair and Just Age of Criminal Responsibility for Youth in New York State,* the NYS Governor's Children's Cabinet Advisory Board states, "New York, a state longconsidered a leader in justice-related issues, is falling behind the vast majority of states on a critical issue—the age of criminal responsibility. While most states treat 16- and 17-year-olds as juveniles, New York treats all 16- and 17-year-olds as adults for criminal responsibility. If arrested after their 16th birthday, they are taken to adult court, spend time detained or do time in local adult jails and can be incarcerated in state run adult correctional institutions if sentenced to longer than one year."

   Moving into New York, where we are working with teen writers in jail, in 2009, a New York State Governors Task Force, along with a Federal Department of Justice investigation exposed system-wide abuse including brutal punishments for minor infractions, failure to provide mental health services, and dangerous restraint tactics that resulted in broken bones, concussions, and lost teeth.

   Incarcerating one juvenile costs approximately $266,000 per year while Alternatives to Detention programs cost as little as $15,000 per youth and have been shown to lower recidivism rates to between 17 and 36% (Correctional Association of New York, 2011). In spite of the very clear facts that youth employment strategies and community based programs geared to youth are the most cost-effective ways to increase public safety, to decrease incarceration rates, and to save taxpayer monies, federal funding for juvenile justice programs has been decreasing steadily since 2002, while more money each year is devoted to expanding the federal prison "industrial" complex.

I Can't Remember the Last Time

Cece Cleveland

Cece has a powerful quiet presence, a demeanor that belies her young age and can easily intimidate until you catch her smile—the smile of a 16-year-old—or are privy to a phrase or two of her dry, quick sense of humor. Once she embraced this writing process, she dropped her guard and her words poured forth and gripped all who heard them, touching the hearts of all who have loved a parent and been abandoned by them. Like other teens struggling with unreliable parents, Cece turned to a gang for family, and is serving state time in prison. While in our group, she shared the circle with another opposing gang member. Through their association in the writing group they moved beyond the dictates of gang protocol and became good friends.

Sometimes *I wish I could run away from the world. I wonder how can I ever gain peace when I run from my past? But I'm afraid of my future. I reflect on childhood memories when ignorance was bliss and around every corner was a new mystery waiting to be explored. In the essence of my innocence lie joy and content. But what happens when the innocence fades and ignorance becomes knowledge of the world's adversities and the coldness of society? You find an adolescent jaded by life, numb to pain and disappointment.*

I can't remember the last time I heard her voice and felt her warm embrace. Damn, is God punishing me? I don't understand why whenever I clench happiness it slowly slips away. In a state of denial I slowly walk toward my closet, never realizing my feet are meeting the ground. I remember this dress. I run my fingers across the fabric recollecting the pearlescent glow of her soft brown eyes. She feels so near to me, but where? She always leaves for a while, but she'll come back.

Every day I sit by the window, awaiting the handful of laughter and soul full of comfort she brings at her arrival. Days go by, weeks, months, and still no sign of her return. The reality of the situation subtly creeps into my circumference sending chills up my spine. I swallow my heart and come to terms with the fact that this time she has left, never to return.

Sometimes I imagine what it's like, death that is. Where do you go? Is it cold, dark and lonely? Is your spirit really at rest? In a drunken fit I pace to and fro contemplating whether or not I want to experience what the non-existence of life is. She was my best friend, my mother. How could I ever withstand the future without her presence? I long to find her, wherever that may be.

I fall into a drunken sleep that night and awake to a sick and twisted dream that seems impossible to break out of. I step off a couch onto the cold floor in a dark and damp room. My instincts know this is not the same place where I laid my head to rest the night before. I panic and scramble to find a light. When my eyes finally adjust to the darkness I realize my familiarity with this place. I realize I am standing in my old two-bedroom basement apartment which I had shared with what was left of my mother. The very place where we settled after my father drove us out of his life like a bad habit. And for what? I was only four. What was so horrible about me that I didn't deserve to be loved the same way every father loved his little girl?

I recline in my chair, break up some bud and twist it up. This is my escape, which soothes the pain and allows me to break free of the memories, break free of the things that clutch my heart like a wrench and haunt the deepest depths of my mind. With every toke I allow part of me to drift away from the darkness I call myself.

I can clearly remember the point in my life that I became cold and unremorseful from being let down and lied to my whole life. I was 12 years old. Like any normal 12-year-old I hated getting up and going to school, but it was made easier awakening to her angelic voice singing in my ear. *"When I look at you, then the world's alright with me."* Till this day I cling to that line of the song she sang to me until the day she died.

"Wake up, Mushy," she said pulling the blanket from over my head.

When I pulled the cover back she began to tickle me.

"Mommy, stop it," I yelled, as I squirmed and giggled. "Okay ma, I'm up!"

Even though I was old enough to pick my own clothes, she always ironed and laid them out for me. By the time I was showered and ready I heard the bus outside. I hugged her and yelled, "Bye, Carrot top!" then jumped over the stairs and out the door.

I always finished my homework before eighth period, so I made plans with my homies for after school. From sitting through a long day of doing more than enough shit I ain't wanna do, I was finally on the bus ride home. I hopped off, made sure there were no scuffs or creases in my Riccz, then pulled out my key and unlocked the door, praying that Mom-dukes made a nigga something to eat. I went upstairs and threw my books in my room.

I heard the TV on in the den, so I walked downstairs to let her know I was home. When I entered the den, to my surprise she wasn't there. So I turned the TV off and ascended the stairs and walked into the kitchen thinking she was there and I hadn't noticed before. Then again, what do you know, she wasn't there either. By now I was really starting to wonder, where the hell could this woman be? Still pondering my thoughts, I retrieved my dog's bowls, fed and gave him water. When I put the cans in the garbage, I noticed it was full. I walked out the back door and down the deck to dispose of the trash. I walked to the side of the house, only to find my mother in the gazebo, almost with her head in her lap, nodded out on pills.

In a pointless effort of trying to wake her, a furious streak of anger engulfed me as I thought to myself, *Why does bullshit like this always happen to me?* In a state of pure rage, I went back into the house and grabbed a Sharpie, a sheet of paper and tape. I returned to the backyard and taped a note to her chest which said, I'M LEAVING, NEVER TO RETURN. THANKS A LOT MOM FOR GETTING CLEAN, and stormed out of the gate, letting it slam behind me.

I've allowed these memories to strip me naked and cast me into a place in time when I look through the haze, and the reflection looking back does not have my name. I am stripped of what I own and what is free. I have nothing to look back at but the person who is not me. And my mother, she was the benevolent force that shackled me to the twisted evils of earth's depths, disallowing my soul passage as I now chase it to the land that is free.

Demons

Patricia McConnell

Patricia had to work hard to drop her guard, to drop what she thought she should write for her teen peers (Hip Hop lyrics), to drop her reticence for speaking her truth in front of an opposing gang member also in our group (they went on to become friends) and to let us into the vulnerable heart of the 11-year-old who'd been forced out onto the street to fend for herself. She spent several months working with us, working in fits and starts into the heart of the writing below. A difficult struggle for Patricia was even imagining breaking her allegiance to the gang that had "parented" her during her life on the streets. As she found the strength of her own voice, we also witnessed her rising confidence to follow her own path. She is still serving time for the actions that brought her to us.

Even *while I'm behind bars, even though I'm not able to do what I want when I want, I'm free behind these bars. I'm free in my heart, free of addiction, free of fear, free of my chains in the outside world. I'm free of the demons who walk, looking for trouble . . .*

Now I'ma go hard. It's time to face the demons inside me. My entire life, there isn't a day that goes by that I don't take at least five minutes from my life to look back to a moment in my past that without a doubt changed me. Whether physically or emotionally, abandonment continues to dwell within the walls of flesh that I call myself.

I really don't like to dwell on the past, but at this point that's where it's gotta go. My mom, she physically abandoned me, mentally fucked me, and emotionally scarred me. My dad, well he chose to cast out his own children for the sake of a woman who physically abused him and mentally got him to the point where he kicked me and my younger brother, his children of eleven and nine out on the streets.

Since I'm a toddler I've been around nothing more than addicts who center their lives around lust and the thrill of their next high and most of all the shiesty plots to get the money to get their fix. From the jump and the first five dollar bill my young seven-year-old hands held onto, I knew that makin' money and flippin' was gonna be one thing I was gonna be good at.

Now at 11, I'm kicked out on the streets due to a fight, like a beat down with my dad's new wife. I knew that I was much smarter than that. I called up my friend John and told him I needed a dub on the arm. Of course he had no problem with it 'cause most of his custies were sent to him by me.

I need to go home, I'm only 11 but I feel so damn grown. He said that he cared then showed me the door. I don't even feel bad I got her blood on the floor dumb whore. You said that "Daddy will always be there."

I feel so alone, you're away and I'm scared, I was so unprepared. I acted purely outta fear. Now I feel like I'm dreaming and you still not here.

Bein' here, it is now that I stand with my head held high, my soul no longer red-eyed and teary. Here I stand tall, towering over this demon after 15 years, with only a few words left to slide off my lips to lay him in his fiery grave. Here I stand strong and say *it's over.* Forever. I've gotta start living for me and not the past. But how, when the past is all I know?

My heart breaks in two when I think about what I put my family through. I think back to a time where there were no tears cried, even moments when tears fell they were easily dried. I see the pain in my grandma's eyes as she says coldly, "This mistake I can't let slide."

I swear I felt my heart stop as I wish I had died, but I held my head high, tried to swallow my pride. Damn, what a ride. How could I think to me the rules didn't apply, nothing to do but think why. I look through this clear Plexiglas wishin' for once that she would lie and say, "It'll be just fine." Tell me, "We'll get through this."

Mentally and physically I'm fit, but emotions are tellin' me "you can't do this." Every day I fight to push through the pain. Some days it's bearable, but other times it's insane. I was raised to never let 'em see you shed a tear. At one point my future felt mapped out. Now it's hazy and unclear.

Here I am at 19-years-old, sitting on a day bed in Riverhead Jail, in the middle of August—August 9th to be exact. It is only now that I realized 100% that the only way I'm gonna get over the past, to get through this is to leave everything, everybody that I've ever known behind.

Secrets, secrets are no fun, especially when they could potentially scar somebody for the rest of their lives. I sit here once again with my mind full of emotions . . . full of questions that I can't answer, questions that people are telling me half-assed answers to that I refuse to believe. Lies, Death, fear and sorrow go hand in hand. More so now, for me that is, that I'm behind bars. Only difference is, now not only am I locked in physically, but I'm locked in mentally. I'm a prisoner in my own mind, trapped in a whirlwind of emotions, of thoughts . . .

"I Thought I Could Bullet-proof You . . ."

Latrice Haywood

"I thought I could bullet-proof you," writes Latrice, who, like so many of the teen girls who end up in jail have given their trust to young men involved in gang life and violence. She joined our group with the encouragement of one of the older women, a surrogate "mother" who had "adopted" her. With little hesitation, Latrice dove into writing this layered love story, pouring out her trauma, grief and remorse in both words and tears. Since her discharge, she has continued to work on it in our Bridges group.

Sunday afternoon, I pull into the driveway, coming from the supermarket with Vonie's mom, niece and nephew. Get out and peep at Vonie sitting in the white jeep across the lot of the building with his cousins. I pick his nephew up and start towards the front door. I usually tell him to come, but he pissed me off earlier. I walk down the hall, past the fire exit and into his apartment, put the baby and the bags down, grab the broom and begin sweeping.

"Ring, ring," his mother's phone goes off.

"Eww," I say. "You need to change this ringtone, Big Ma." That's what we call his mom, Big Ma. Me thinking nothing of the phone call, I pick it up.

"Hello? . . . Helloo?"

"Babe is that you?" he asks nervously.

"Yeah, it's me, Vonie, what's wrong?"

"Call the cops," he yells.

I immediately call and run outside. First thing I see is little kids, little toddlers, no older than three, running towards the gate about

30 feet opposite the front door. I run out to the parking lot and see about 30 guys surround the jeep. Every single one has a bat, knife, steel pole or a stick, all but two. These two look different from them all. These two have big black hoodies on and have guns pointed towards the jeep. I know all 30 of them.

I begin to hear shots—four consistent ones and five after them like firecrackers. I run towards them. The tall dark-skinned male with big lips has a gun pointed to Vonie's head. I scream, the dark-skinned one flinches and lets off the last shot. I close my eyes as if I am seeing things. But it is as real as the stunned look on my face. Someone yells in a deep raspy voice, "There's Latrice, take flight." And they do. They all do. I take three more steps and the driver's side door where he was sitting, opens. He steps out and immediately falls to his knees.

White bright lights beeping and the buzzing of machines and the smell of Purell hand sanitizer in the air. I'm at Huntington Hospital. I'm looking around for familiar faces, but I see none. All I see are a bunch of women in blue and white scrubs. In the emergency department, distraught, out of breath, sweaty, teary-eyed and confused, running from room to room looking for him. A nurse approaches me with a concerned look on her face and asks if I need help. I can tell she is Dominican by her accent and dark skin tone.

"I'm looking for Davon. Davon White, he was shot, where is he, is he okay?"

"Ma'am, I need you to calm down," the nurse says.

But I can't. "He's allergic to Bacitracin, don't give him that . . . and bananas too, don't feed him that. Where is he?" The tears start to flow harder as she walks me over to the tan front desk, messy with papers.

"He's coming out of surgery now," she says handing me a blue tissue.

"No!" I scream. "You put him to sleep? You can't give him anesthetics he has asthma!"

What if he doesn't wake up? I think. There I go again, thinking of the worst-case scenario.

"There he is, being rolled into room three," she says, interrupting my jumbled thoughts

I dash towards the room. I walk into what looks like a white box with a whole bunch of machines beeping consistently. There he is . . . looks to be okay, lying flat on his back covered in what looks like thirty blankets. I walk over to his right side and grab his cold, dark, rough hand.

"Vonie . . . Vonie, look at me," I say sobbing already and the man didn't say two words yet.

He looks up, gripping my hand tighter and says faintly, "Babe."

"Yes, Vonie, I'm here."

His eyes begin to close, and his grip loosens.

"Hold my hand, Von!" I begin to panic.

"Hold my hand," I repeat. He looks up and holds my hand.

"I love you," he says.

"I love you too," I say, as tears fall on his white knitted blankets. He begins to drift back to sleep. I figure it's the morphine he's on. As he sleeps, I stare as I wipe the sweat off his brown dark forehead, touching his big lips and patting his rough black hair with the look of agony on my face.

I begin to hear heavy footsteps, getting closer and closer, reminding me of the Tims my father wore. I look towards the door and there is a white, blue-eyed, freckle-faced detective in a blue shirt, about 6'5" with khakis standing on the threshold.

He looks at me. "You have to leave," he demands.

"What!" I snap at him. I hate when people tell me what I have to do.

"I'd like to speak with Davon alone," he says hesitantly.

I look back at Davon. We wake him. I tell him I love him once more.

As the DT walks closer towards me, he begins to nudge me.

"Don't touch me, and don't rush me," I say, cold and harsh as my face turns towards him. Davon grabs my hand tightly and says, "I love you too."

He releases my hand and I walk back out to the door. I pause and glance back at Von and say to myself, *I thought I could bulletproof you.* Walking back through the lobby out the sliding doors. At this point, all the tears have stopped, but my heart rate is still accelerating. Thinking back to that "suicide incident" last week . . .

November 23

After a day of tit for tats, unnecessary attitudes, smart comments and hurt feelings I remain silent. This argument has gotten old the third time around. *Yeah I cheated—three years ago—we're still on this—why?* But I never got up the guts to say this outside my thoughts. I'd just sit and stare as he roared like a wild beast.

Nostrils flaring—"Jennifer, you have a whore for a daughter-in-law!" he would yell.

"D.C. Stop talkin' to that girl that way."

He'd woken his mom once again at 2 A.M. with his B.S. I didn't want to deal with it—I hated myself for it—I didn't expect him to forgive me until I forgave myself. Damn, low self-esteem kickin' in so once again, I ran. As he was in the bathroom carrying on to his mom while she was try'na calm him down, I grabbed my cheetah print duffle bag and stuffed all my shit inside. I'd come back for the heavy shit, I figured. But all my clothes I took.

He opened the bedroom door with disgust in his eyes . . . I stepped up on the brown post at the far corner of the bed, hopped onto the ledge and out the window of his first floor apartment. Walked a mile home in the dark from First Avenue to Tenth Avenue. When I got to my tan two-story home, I didn't walk in. I sat on the blue cobblestone stoop, gazing at the stars trying to escape reality with the distractions of astronomy.

Five minutes later my phone vibrated consistently for 20 seconds straight. I knew who it was and definitely what it was—angry break-up texts.

"I hate you, don't ever want to see you again, I deserve better. Five years of you and I should've learned, I can't trust a bitch like you—I'ma find a new wife."

This was nothing new to me. I'd learned to deal with his temper tantrums and verbal abuse for a while. I felt I deserved it. I was wrong to hurt him the way I did.

I wrote back, "I'm coming home." Then turned my phone off—I knew he was opposed. It was late, cold and scary out. Dark and foggy, like a scene from a scary movie. All I heard was the sound of T.V. on the inside and faint crickets. I got up and walked inside . . . up six steps to the hallway, Jayden's room dead ahead and on the right my mom's room . . . a little farther down-mine . . . I threw the bag down the hall—it landed in my room.

Walked back down to the front door and took the keys to my mom's midnight blue Honda off the key hook and headed out, locking the door behind me. Got in the car and headed back to First Avenue doin' 80 through the dark quiet streets of the South Side. Pulled into the parking lot of the apartment building anxious and dizzy. As I parked the car I felt so lightheaded, my mind going 100 mph but focused on the one thing. Von. I got out and started towards the door. When I got to the front door I called his 14-year-old niece, Jada.

"Hello?" Push the button to open the front door.

"What's wrong?"

"Please, Jada."

"It's open."

I hung up and walked to the end of the hall and there he was—not surprised to see me but not happy either. I followed him into the house. He was on the phone talking to Quae, my cousin. Not really payin' me any mind. He hung up with Quae and walked back out into the building's hallway, me two steps behind.

Walking close as he made his way back to the front door, he stopped and turned to face me. "What do you want?" he said.

I stared into his bloodshot red eyes as he waited for a response clenching his jaw though I froze silent and still as a statue. He turned to leave and I blurted out, "Where are you going?"

"To the store, why?"

"What, what, what do you want from me?" he yelled.

"Lemme drive you."

"No, I'll walk."

"Either way, I'm coming."

"You're a nuisance!"

"And you're stubborn!" Am I complaining?"

"Leave."

"No!"

"I don't want you!"

"We go through this constantly . . . you don't mean, watch what you say this time. I'm so close to the edge, I'ma snap."

He stepped closer to me, face to face—well, chest to face—and he said "I'm done."

"The day you leave is the day I die—remember that?"

"Man fuck that, I wish you would."

"You don't care remember, so lemme grant your wish."

I ran out the front door and back into the car. He followed and sat in the passenger seat.

"Leave me alone, I'm gone. Just like you wanted, word to it all you won't see me again and you're not invited to my funeral bitch . . . fuck out of my car."

"I wasn't planning on coming!" he laughed.

"Let me go or close the door—shit, nigga, you wanna come too?" I yelled. "I'm tired of you—of you treating me this way, I deserve so much more, my father be so disappointed to see what I'm putting up with."

"Yeah, he'd also be disappointed to know that nigga was between your . . . " He stopped as I stared and shook my head. I'm sayin'—if looks could kill.

Right then he took the keys out my hand.

"I'm getting off this earth one way or another," I said staring at the house keys sticking out his sweat pants pocket. I opened the car door in preparation for what I was about to do. I quickly snatched the house keys and ran. I got through the front door of the house and headed for the stairs (the elevator would take too long) running up three flights, hearing his close footsteps behind me, his pace picking up as he realized my goal.

The staircase got narrow. It led to the roof access door, cautioned with red signs reading "Do not enter" and "Restricted."

Vonie yelled, "Stop!" but I kept going. He yanked the hood of my grey Abercrombie sweatshirt to restrain me. It didn't work. I ran faster and faster—I'm now sweating, legs are cramping and tears are flowing. I got to the door and pushed it open. It was now raining, the roof was slippery. I ran and found a metal chair I threw behind me to place in his way. Step after step closer to the edge, splashing in puddles on the dirty white rooftop I began to see the green of the grass more and more. I reached the edge and pivoted staring at Davon still struggling with the metal chair that got caught on his sweatpants. I screamed out, "I love you," trying to pierce through the loud raring of the sky's thunder. My face soaking, not able to differentiate between tears or raindrops all in the matter of three seconds I stretched my arms out and leaned back, closing my eyes waiting for the moment my pain would vanish.

Unexpectedly I felt him grab me right after most of my body weight was shifted backwards, pulling me from the edge back to the middle of the roof. He just hugged me apologizing repetitively,

"I do love you, I do, I can't live without you—why would you try to do this?" he asked.

"You told me to leave! You told me you didn't want me, I'd rather die a thousand deaths than deal with the pain I caused you, I'm sorry—I'm so sorry."

Then it started to pour as we sat in the middle of a rooftop puddle. I was never one used to admitting mistakes—I would run away from them, thinking they'd disappear. But this was the moment I'd realized that this conflict was internal and I had been trying to escape my own mind.

If he would've let go—he would've never got shot.

Pain

Deidre Jackson

When women come into Herstory, whether they are behind bars or living outside, we ask them to imagine that they are writing a book in which gradually their lives will unfold. The exercise of finding the "Page One Moment" becomes a trigger for beginning to tell a story, leading to chapter after chapter and page after page. Jackson, as Deidre preferred to call herself, presented a tough and guarded picture when she came into our group, but the person who emerges on the page is quite different. Intermingling prose poems and prayers through these short chapters that trace her journey away from her first foster home into a life of her own choice, she gives us a vivid picture of a 14-year-old coming of age in the tragically uncaring atmosphere of "the hood," looking for power, mastery of the world that she has been thrown into, and ultimately for a relief and tenderness not to be easily found. The magic of this story is the vulnerability she displays, even while we watch her harden and toughen into being able to cope with the life she is given. It is in her spirit and her search that we begin to contemplate what healing might be possible when our stories begin to connect the dots.

If you looked into my life you'll see what I have seen, go where I have gone and feel what I have felt. My eyes have hurt me more than my ears, but my heart is the one that has been hurt the most.

You see me then you think you know me but have no idea. You hear what people say then you judge me, which I don't care.

Who am I, why I act the way I act, all I know, what I been through, what I see, how I feel, why I don't trust and why I hate with passion is because of the pain.

I am angry, I hate, I curse, I don't love, I punch, I spit and I will kill because I hurt and am in so much pain. All I know, all my life, don't want you to care, don't wanna see no shed tears. Just want you to know who I am.

Abandoned, beaten, betrayed, hurt, hit, judged, molested, picked on, raped, lied to, lied on is mostly what I battle with from day in and day out. With all of this on my brain I then have to cope with people which I can't, 'cause I don't want to. People/humans are made to hurt and cause pain so when I can I turn to nature. Nature—the trees, green grass and water—soothes me. I feel more at peace when alone. Do I trust myself? Yes, only when I'm alone.

(1)

I think I'm making the right decision, I know I'm making the right decision. These are the things that are going through my head as I am walking down the block, a bag full of clothes, freezing my ass off. I really don't wanna leave Ms. Best, because she is my mother, the only woman I call Ma, or Mommy. Over the past 11½ years she has been good to me. Yes I've had my ass whooped, but I deserved it.

Mommy is on dialysis and is very weak. She is dying soon so I refuse to be living under the roof of the rest of these abusive people! I hate them. All they do is beat on me, embarrass me, talk shit to me and make me cry . . . I mean Ms. Best could discipline me, 'cause she is the one who took me in, the only one who really loves me and the one who is my foster parent. But now Ms. Best is getting too sick and she can't even speak up for me and when she does they be hating . . . So I don't know why they are always trying to be my mothers.

These are the things that are going through my head as I am going to this new home. I really don't want to go, but I'm 14-years-old now and when she is dead and gone I will not be left with them, they will not treat me the same . . .

So here I am freezing, rolling my valuables down a street in the ice cold October weather saying bye to my old neighborhood, "Bed Stuy," and hello to the new foster home, Ms. Inez Lindsay.

(2)

"Hello Ms. Lindsay this is Deidra. Did the agency notify you to let you know I was coming? Okay, well I'm not sure of where you live could you let me know the address? Okay, I'll call you if I get lost. Thanks, good-bye."

I just got finished talking to the new foster mother with the directions to the new foster home. I hope this home is better. I hope she allows me to shop with my own money. I hope I get new sneakers. Thank God it's still in Brooklyn. That way I could still visit Ms. Best and my friends. Hopefully I could have a little bit of freedom to do any of these things.

I arrived at the house.

"Hello, Ms. Lindsay, I'm Deidra."

"Well, come in and you make me seem old by calling me Ms. Lindsay. Just call me Shoogi."

Shoogi lived across the tracks, which is Crown Heights in Brooklyn, in a house. I came from a house, so I was familiar with house duties and chores. I just hoped I wouldn't be a slave. Shoogi escorted me to my room, which was big. It had a sink in it and I had the front window. I was hype 'cause I had a room before, but it was never this big, and this even had an extra bed—not to share, but for company if I made friends. The best part of this room was that I had a door for privacy and I could play music. Shoogi told me to unpack and when I'm done if I'm hungry I could get something to eat and meet the rest of the family.

As I unpacked I was thinking of so many things and how my life would change dramatically just by all this freedom. What I wondered most was, *Will this be the end of my journey—Will she treat me right? Will she love me like Ms. Best?*—and if she was abusive, 'cause that was the rap! *No one will put their hands on me again.*

As I went out to go downstairs, I turned back to close the door. I looked out the window and noticed how cloudy it was. Is it a dark cloud like this all the time? Well I don't care cause this is the life right now! Freedom, what every teenager should have. As I went out the door and thanked God for this home, I was thinking about Ms. Best, missing her already, but pushed it to the side 'cause I had a decision that had to be made and I believe it was a good one—so I thought.

(3)

I left Boys & Girls H.S. and started going to Sarah J. Hale. I could have stayed at the High but I just wanted to be in a whole new environment, period. Ms. Lindsay turned out to be different, real different. I was able to do whatever I wanted, could stay out to 12 A.M., if not stay where I'm at—*Don't come in the house high*—so basically for a 14-year-old it was the life for me. I was hanging outside more and met the neighborhood. I was a pleasant kid. Instead of being popular I was "popping." I guess people liked me 'cause I was eager to learn about the streets and my surroundings. I was never scared, I was in fights, a go-getter, and my friend and I were loyal to each other. We never let anything happen to each other. My life was wild and crazy. It was headed in the wrong direction right before my eyes and I didn't even realize it 'cause I was so young, plus I was having fun.

Well anyway, one day while in the house I met Nicole. Nicole was Shoogi's daughter-in-law. Shoogi loved Nicole and I could see why. They were cut from the same cloth. Anyway, Shoogi had a son who was in jail and couldn't come home until he at least did 15 years. He had a lot of street cred and everybody knew this nigga.

Well, Nicole was cool, she was 12 years older than me at 26, and chose to be around me. She tried to get me in clubs, which worked sometimes. She made her runs in the hood with me riding shotgun, she brung me to her house and let me chill with her smoking and drinking what I wanted and doing what I wanted. Nicole always had money, always smelled good, was fresh and always wore a lot of jewelry.

One day I was sitting on the stoop and Nicole said, "Deidra I'll be back."

"Where you going?" I asked.

She said, "Out. I'm going out shopping."

I said, "I wanna go," thinking to myself, *Who wouldn't wanna go shopping and why she acting funny for?* So then Shoogi came in front of the door from the inside and Nicole looked at Shoogi like getting permission through eye contact and I believe Shoogi gave it to her and I was happy because Nicole said, "Let's go."

That day—I believe it was winter and almost spring around March—when I was 14, was the beginning of my life being changed. To Nicole and Shoogi I was a pawn, a money-maker, young and crazy with drive and something to prove. To me during that time I was the happiest person on earth to be going shopping.

That day, when I think about it, it was the day shopping would become a drug, far worse than dope. The clothes was cool and money gave me a rush. So basically I was hooked/an addict to the fast life at an early age and got hooked in a foster home.

That day my life changed for the worst and it was the beginning of my life being ruined.

(4)

"Deidra, we going to Staten Island Mall and you must listen."

Of course I was gonna listen, I wanted new clothes. I never had anyone who ever wanted to take me shopping, let alone take me all the way to Staten Island to do it.

Well, when I got there to the mall it was amazing. I went shopping before but not to a mall and not to get anything I wanted, especially if it was name brand. I was told to hold two Gap bags. The bags were empty and I looked at Nicole. She must have read my mind 'cause she said she will fill them up and I was to leave the store and wait for her at the same exit we came in.

I did that and made it in and out of every store w/o being detected about ten times. By the time we finished we had two black garbage bags filled with merchandise on the Staten Island ferry. Nicole was impressed with me. She didn't have to tell me much. I was smooth when it came to getting in and getting out of the stores, and I had a baby face, which worked in my favor. If anything happened, all I had to do was call Shoogi or Nicole and they would come to the precinct and get me. Nicole was creating a monster and was excited 'cause of the money she was about to make.

When Myquan appeared, he and Nicole started busting down the items two ways. My things were in Nicole's pile. They were asking me my size in jeans, shirts and coats. I was so shocked and happy at the same time, but I kept it to myself and acted nonchalant about the whole situation.

Everyday was a good day for me and every boosting team was trying to cut Nicole's throat to have me on their team. It was like

I was already seasoned and I didn't talk much, plus the fact I didn't ask for much. They gave me new clothes, extra to sell, plus $200 for pocket money, but at the end of the day whatever they gave me they had double. I was just for once happy. I was fresh to death cute with paper in my pocket. I was doing better than any 14-year-old around. In school I was getting attention but I even stopped going 'cause I started chasing money and kept up to date with the latest wears. I was like a walking mannequin in the hood 'cause the way people used to window shop and gawk at the latest fashions in the store windows that they could never afford was the same way they used to look at me. Little did I know I was being used. I started to get a name around the hood. Every time I would see older hustlers, they would ask what I got or just give me their numbers. All the teens wanted to be my friend and in that way I was being used to recruit others. They would see how fresh I was and want to be down. Others just used to be hating on me and wanted to fight me and I would. I made a couple of examples and wasn't fucked with, or the one to be fucked with.

After that I just started chilling with the older people. I never cliqued with the younger people my age anyway 'cause they weren't on my level and they weren't about nothing—at least nothing I was into and I was into money. I was able to be a teenager but very little. When nobody was around that was the only time I had to myself so I started hanging out with this girl Sandra. I was attracted to her at first because she looked just like Foxy Brown but better. She was gorgeous.

Now that I am older I can understand what I was going through. I first met her at my corner store and I asked her was she related to Foxy and she said, "No."

I said, "You look just like her" and we introduced ourselves and that was the beginning of our friendship.

(5)

Back at Shoogi's house, shit was kinda getting crazy. First of all Shoogi was a drunk. She used to go to church every Sunday and her brother was even a pastor at the church, but after service was over she used to send me to the store to get her Bud—a 40-ounce and a six-pack—and yes, they used to sell it to me. Well anyway Shoogi used to be in the house getting twisted, and once I came in the house all hell broke loose. Every time I came in at the wrong time, trying to satisfy my hunger from the chocolate weed I just smoked. She used to sit me in the living room questioning me for two to three hours, asking me have I smoked, over and over again, thinking my answer would change from no. Truth is, if I was high, she just blew it and she knew she did.

So I just started going to my friend Sandra's crib and her grandmom's used to always have some shit cooking on the stove. Sandra's grandmoms lived in the projects, Albany Projects, and it was always something going on there, but once you got on the inside of Sandra's grandmom's house it was a different story. It was peaceful and I just felt like I belonged.

Sandra turned into my best friend and we started doing everything together. I was in love with her and used to give her half of whatever I had. Not only 'cause she didn't have it, but because I secretly treated her like a girl I was seeing. At the time, I really didn't know about the life, but I knew I was feeling something for her and she was feeling something for me. But I didn't wanna speak on it, 'cause I didn't know how to, plus I didn't know what I was to say. I learned about my feelings years later. I didn't even know what I was going through until I learned about it in the streets where I learned everything.

Sandra stuck to me like glue, but I didn't want her doing what I was doing like stealing, smoking, and not going to school 'cause her family was feeding me and I didn't want them to believe I was influencing her in a bad way. Sandra really liked me and she always had my back and would curse and beat up anybody for me, but I would never want her to be in a war with me and her family. I would never put her in that predicament to have to choose, and that is why I told her, "Don't let me start you doing anything, do it 'cause you want to. Be your own person."

From that day on she respected me and put me onto liquor and told me that's how she got high and not to tell her brothers or sisters. Everywhere I was, Sandra wasn't far, and one day Myquan saw her and wanted to know who she was, and I told him as well as the brothers she had that I would fuck him up if he even thought about it. We were 14 and 15 and he was 26 and that was old to us because we were virgins. So Myquan I guess thought about it and left it alone for now.

Trust U? Why should I? U R a snake in nice clothes, U smile in my face and plot behind my back. U R not a friend of mine and could never be. I know people like U, all my life I've dealt with people like U and all my life I've seen people just like you. U act like my friend but I see through U. U R not my friend. I put my guard down around U but U just R plotting to hurt me. I despise U. U think I don't know what's going on? Well I do, I know everything and it's best I stay away from u, that is why I keep my grass cut short so I can see people like u a mile away even with my bad eye sight and all. U R no different from the others that is why I recognized who u were from when I first looked into your eyes.

Back to the streets things started to get crazy. I was officially on Myquan's team 'cause I wanted more and Myquan gave it to me. Nicole was hating on me. She got three 19- and 20-year-olds to pour bleach in my eyes and jump me. I guess she was hurt because I screamed on her and offered her to fight and she backed down.

I guess Nicole was embarrassed 'cause my little self wasn't scared of her, so she did what any project chick would have done. Shoogi was riding with Nicole, because she didn't like Myquan anyway from the beef her son had with him, so I left Shoogi. I had a couple of choices which were to go to a group home upstate, be with my crackhead mom, go back to the Best family or stay with Sandra and be in the hood still getting fly and getting money. Which one do you think I chose?

(6)

I chose the fast life. The money, the clothes and the cars would come later. I stayed with Sandra and her family. I had no rules to follow and I could do whatever I wanted. My life became a routine. Get up, smoke me some weed, which would relax me, shower, pop tags, get dressed and get ready to get money. When I came back from getting money it was usually the same: Sell my items stash my money, then bullshit around the hood. I became addicted to popping tags and if I wanted to pop tags every day I would have to go out to get it every day.

The more I went out hustling, the more I became better as a professional thief. Myquan was slick. He taught me everything I knew. I didn't say much—all I had to do was watch him. If I saw something that I wanted, he would get it, no matter if it was chained down, locked down, high up in the ceiling, in the managers' faces or even in their hands. Whatever it was he was able to get it. He was 27, but he looked much older than his years. He was a nice dressing man with a big ass head covered with long braids. He had some big ass hands like the hulk, so if he grabbed anything he was able to grab enough of it. He had been doing this since 15, so he knew a lot that I needed to learn and I did learn it. That's why as of today I could smell an undercover officer and sense trouble.

I was a good listener, so I knew a little something about him, at least the things he didn't tell me like not knowing the time unless it was digital, and I soon learned he couldn't count money as fast as I could, so with a little fast talking I was able to beat him out of a $100 here and there, but in all actuality I was taking my money back.

(7)

Back to the living conditions with Sandra was cool. I came and went as I pleased and didn't have to answer to no one. Like I said before, I was raised in a house so I had manners. All Sandra grand-moms was concerned about was: she don't want no one poppin' up pregnant under her roof or else you got to go! She did not have to worry about that, 'cause that was the furthest thing away from my mind. A dude couldn't do anything that I couldn't do for myself. Besides these dudes were broke, and only wanted one thing, and from me they weren't getting it.

Everywhere me and Sandra went guys would chase behind us. Sandra was 5'4", wore a size 27 in female's jeans, small to petite, dark brown smooth complexion, naturally arched eyebrows, pretty teeth, nice smile and long hair that she wore in a dubie. Me, on the other hand, I wore size 30 in female jeans, medium top, with long hair that I also wore in a dubie. So dudes would always ask or mistake us for sisters, thinking in their heads it would be some sort of double dating going on. I would immediately shut them down letting them know I got a man and his name is B.F. I just laughed in their face 'cause me and Sandra knew my B.F stood for that dead president, Benjamin Franklin.

After a while I just started wearing looser clothes 'cause guys got on my nerves at the way they just stared at your backside. So I just started the Aaliyah look, wearing loose pants and tight shirts with shades over my eyes. Still that didn't stop the attention—guys actually thought that was sexy. I figured they must have had a real crush on the singer Aaliyah. So I just started wearing men's clothes period. Not too big, not too small, just men fitted clothes that kept the men at bay. Now instead of saying, "Shawty what's ur name?" they would say, "Sandra who dat?" Scared to even say anything to me thinking I would bite their neck off. Sandra would wonder what was up with the transformation, but would never ask. Her sisters and brothers did, but I ignored them. I just despised men—they think with their dicks only. They rape, molest and disrespect women all day, everyday, then expect you to be like pudding in their hands. I just didn't and still don't have the patience for them.

(8)

With Myquan things started to change and so did I. Not only did I start to dress like a man, but I also thought like one. Myquan started to feel threatened so he did the ultimate. We were in this store and he was tryna put some coats in my bag while the sales lady was staring right at us. Not only was she staring at us, but the manager came upstairs from the basement. So as soon as he and Myquan locked eyes, they had a race and Myquan got out. So I was left in the store and they kept me there and called the cops. I was scared to death. I didn't know what was gonna happen because I didn't even know about nobody in jail.

Remember, I came from Ms. Best house where I never knew about anything ('cause we never went outside) about being exposed to the world. I was naïve to a lot of this but like I said before, I caught on quick. The cops arrived and one officer stood near me asking me questions while the other officer was with the store manager and the saleswoman.

"How old are you?"

I said, "14."

So he then asked, "Where do you live? Do you have any I.D.?"

I said I lived in Brooklyn and the only I.D. I had was my school I.D. They took a look at my I.D. and held it until they finished with the manager. After they finished with the manager they escorted me to the cop car. When I got there I was crying like a baby. I started saying things like, "Please don't take me to jail, if my mother finds out she is gonna beat me. Please, Mr. Officer, please, God help me, I'm gonna be in trouble. I swear I am not gonna be in that store or no other store again."

A few minutes later the officer stopped the car. When I looked around we were on a public block. His partner got out of the car opened the back door and said, "Get out of here, kid." He passed me my I.D. and said, "Stay out of trouble. Today is your lucky day. Next time it won't be like this."

I hurried up and got out the car and went to the train station that they dropped me off in front of. I got on the train, thinking of a story to tell them, 'cause if I told them the real story they would not have believed me.

When I got back to the hood my anger surfaced when I saw Myquan. He was chilling, hanging out, joking and laughing, while I could have lost my freedom. I got so upset 'cause I felt I was not that important and while my life could have been put on hold, his just went on. As soon as I got up on him, I asked, "Why the fuck you leave me for dead in that store?"

He couldn't say nothing but, "How did you make it out?"

All I knew was I blacked out and 2pc'd him. One fist to the mouth and the left hook in his jawbone. I knew he could beat me, but he had to know just like everyone else who was standing around that I was no slouch. With that 2pc he didn't stagger, but I drew blood so after that we locked ass. He got the best of me, but I stood my ground. After what seemed like a long five minutes some dudes broke it up, yelling at him once they saw he was fighting a little girl. When we were finally separated I told him, "It's not over," and headed towards the projects to Sandra's grandmom's.

On my way to Sandra's all the dudes who knew me and of me were asking me, "Are you okay?"

I said, "Yeah, why you ask?"

Then they pointed at my shirt. I had Myquam's blood on me from when I punched him in the mouth. I told them I was good and if I needed them I'd holla. No sooner when I got inside the crib the phone was ringing. Sandra answered it while asking me was I okay. I told her, 'Yeah, why?" then remembered the blood that was on my clothes.

"Yeah, who is it? " Sandra said into the phone. It must have been for me, 'cause Sandra looked my way. I said, "Who is it?" And she said, "Myquan." I told her to give me the phone.

"Yo, what the fuck do you want, 'cause I'm on my way back down there for round two."

"You, Deidra, you need to calm down."

"Don't tell me what to do! I do as I please now. What the fuck u call up here for?"

"Yo, I'm sorry . . . my bad."

"Yeah, you sorry alright." Then I hung up the phone. I was pissed off. That punk motherfucker wasn't sorry, not the least bit. There he goes only thinking about himself. He was not sorry, back at that store when he purposely left me for dead. He didn't care about no one but himself, and since I was young, liked clothes and money, for him it was like a kid at Toys R Us.

I walked in the back, into me and Sandra's room and got undressed. When I was naked with nothing but my 34B bra and my medium underwear Sandra began to giggle. I stopped my train of thought and brung my attention to Sandra giggling.

I said, "What's so funny?"

She said, "You."

"And what's so funny about me?"

"You act and dress like a straight dude, but now you look like a straight bitch in your Vicki Secrets."

I looked at myself in the mirror and we both began to laugh.

"I see I have to make some changes then."

"Nah, not really, I love who you are and you are very beautiful . . . I mean as a girl."

I left it at that and began to run the hot water so I could soak. I got into the water, but not before locking and stuffing the bottom of the door with a towel. Then I began to roll up some weed. As I took a pull of it, I contemplated on my life and how in less than a year it had changed. I thought about Ms. Best and how she was doing. I thought of why she kept me in the house. I thought about how I would never in a million years would have been able to enjoy my life like this if I would have stayed there, but I also thought about how I would have been going to school and I thought about family. I was on my own, there would be no more family get-togethers for me, no more Thanksgivings with family I was raised by, no more Christmases or cookouts, no more nothing. Was it worth giving all that up just to rip and run the streets, wear the most expensive clothes and the latest sneakers, and smoke the best weed? Yes . . . Yes, it was to a 14-year-old who never had nothing.

(9)

It was midway through October 1996 and I created a buzz in the streets. My summer was spectacular and my winter was gonna be the same. Me and my new crew of four 16- and 17-year-olds tore up the stores. People started to put in orders and we used to fill them. We were almost on the same level as the old heads, but not quite. I didn't want too much attention on me anyway, 'cause then the stuck-up kids would have guns in our faces in a millisecond. I was still 14-years-old and doing my thing. I had Auirex leather coats, Guess jeans, suits, Ralph Lauren knitted sweaters, Tommy Hilfiger everything, Gortex boots, Polo boots, a pocket full of cash and a draw full as a stash. I was getting taller so I was slimmer than before wearing a 31/32 in men's jeans rather than a 33/34.

I still wore a men's medium sweater but could pull off a men's small, depending on the maker. I smoked weed . . . a lot of it so that kept my weight down plus running the streets helped out. I still wore my hair in a ponytail blow-dried out by the Dominicans, but now it was covered by a baseball cap from whatever designer outfit I wore. So if I wore a Diesel outfit, I had on a Diesel hat, Armani Exchange w/Armani Exchange, Polo with Polo so forth so on, but on my off days I rocked Nautica sweatsuit, some Air Max and a Yankee fitted cap. I had four top teeth covered by gold caps, but mine were frames with diamonds around each of them, gold balls in my ears and a 16″ herringbone chain on my neck. I was doing quite alright for myself.

I woke up on this particular day and I was hungrier than a hostage. I jumped up, took a quick shower, got dressed in a grey Nautica Competition sweat suit, red Nautica Competition vest, a white nautical T-shirt, some grey, red and white Air Max and an Angel red and white fitted cap, rolled me up some weed, put it into my pocket as well as the money that I had in my other pants pocket. I called our neighborhood cab, 'cause that's the only cabbie that allows us to smoke or drink while we ride for a tip. When cabbie arrived, I told him to take me to the best Spanish restaurant Brooklyn has. After 20 minutes, I reached this Spanish restaurant. It was in East New York, a rough part in Brooklyn. Thank God I left my jewelry, because these niggas looked thirsty out here and I didn't have my bitch cutter on me.

I told cabbie I was gonna call him when I was done and gave him

$20. I went into the restaurant and ordered my favorite Spanish dish and sat down. The lady brung my food to me, and no sooner than she left I started pigging out.

"Can I take this seat?" A chick voice I heard. I just stared at her.

She said, "the chair, table seat . . . Can I sit here with you? There is no other table available."

I said, "Sure, let me just get this out of your way."

She started giggling.

I said, "What's funny?"

And she said, "You seem to be dropping and spilling everything except for that piece of pork on your fork."

I gave her a half smile, knowing she was right.

I said, "I'm getting my money's worth," and smiled.

I asked her what she was ordering and she said, "Chicken soup."

I said, "Chicken soup."

She said, "Yeah, did I say it right?"

I said, "Yeah, but you could of got Campbell's, if you wanted some chicken soup."

She gave me the evil eye, explaining the difference between Spanish and Campbell's chicken soup. She even let me taste a little, once it came. It was awesome.

She said, "By the looks of things, you like what you just tasted, so don't be judging things you didn't give a try."

I said, "Thanks for the info."

I asked, "What is your name?" and she said "Nubushe." She asked me mine and I told her. We started talking and I started to enjoy the conversation. Then she asked me, was I a lesbian?

I said, "Lesbian? What is that?"

She looked at me like I was playing, then I said, "Nah, I'm for real. What is that?"

Then she went on to explain how a lesbian is a female who likes other females.

I said, "No, what makes you think that?

She said, "Well first of all you are dressed in men clothes, and with that baseball cap on, you look like a dude from the back." We started to talk more, and then after an hour she left. I didn't know how fast time could go by, but it did. After she left I got my things ready and got on the phone to call cabbie. I had plans for today as I waited for cabbie.

I cleaned up my mess and I stopped when I saw an unusual napkin. It wasn't unusual, but it wasn't the ones the restaurant gave us—it was from Dunkin Donuts. I knew I didn't have Dunkin Donuts so what was it doing on the table, 'cause it wasn't there before? I looked at it, and it was the girl Nubushe's number on it. And it said, "Call me if you want to be friends." She must have wrote it when I got a refill on my iced tea, but why couldn't she just hand me her number instead of being secretive? That will just have to wait 'til I speak to her. A horn honking brought me back to reality. It was cabbie.

The ride back, I finished the rest of my weed and thought about Nubushe. She was fine and by the way she talked I could tell she was smart. I had to check myself, 'cause I caught myself fantasizing about her. What was going on? Maybe it was the weed playing tricks on me . . . or maybe it wasn't.

I love you so much, but don't know how to show it. Sometimes I show it in crazy ways. Sometimes I neglect you, maybe I don't love you, I'm just learning. I take away from you, just to give to others. I put others before you, only to see others happy, even if I'm suffering. I let my guard down, only to get hurt. Every time that happens, it is a hard time to get back on my feet. I should take the time out to get to know you, but where would I start? You are a decent person that someone could easily love, but you are so angry that you don't allow no one in, afraid to get hurt. I love you, but I'm loving you from a distance, which is not okay ' cause you are all I got.

(10)

I went back to Sandra's and put on some decent clothes. A Diesel sweater, some Diesel jeans, some Zara sneakers, a Zara leather jacket, put my hair in a ponytail and put a Zara hat over my ponytail. I went to go get some more money out my stash and went outside. The first thing I had to do was get a $10 roll of quarters to call Nubushe. I chose the pay phone 'cause I didn't want Sandra or no one hustling in my conversation with her. I wanted to talk to her and let her know how I felt or how I've been feeling about my sexuality. I got my quarters from the Laundromat and headed to a phone. On my way to the phone, I saw Myquan and he blocked my path from walking. Every time I would walk, he'd get in the way.

"Come on, Deidra. You gonna stay mad at me forever?"

"I might, I haven't thought about it yet. Now get out of my way."

"So you not fucking with me no more? You not my friend no more? You don't know how to appreciate a friend. Yo, Deidra I'm sorry, please just call me, I wanna get some money with you. "

"I'll think about it. Now just move out my way, so I can do more important things."

After I finished talking to Myquan, I went to call Nubushe.

"Hello, can I speak to Nubushe? "

"This is she."

"Well, this is Deidra . . . "

Nubushe and I talked for a while—through five dollars worth of quarters—before she asked me to come over to her house. I asked her where she lived, wrote the address down, then hung up the phone. I was thinking of the things I had to do on that day and figured, I'll just chill with Nubushe. I had a couple of thousands in the stash and a couple of hundreds in my pockets, so to me that was good. Plus I had four garbage bags filled with clothes in Sandra's closet and a closet rack filled with leathers of every color, plus goose down vests. Good thing Sandra had two closets in her room or else I didn't know where all that shit would go.

I called the houses of my other crew members and told them, "Don't wait on me, because I can't make it." They were shocked but happy cause they wanted to chill out that day also—only to show off their clothes and spend up their money. My next call went out to cabbie, I needed him to take me cause I wasn't too familiar with Canarsie and didn't want to get beat in the head. Then I bumped into Sandra.

"Where were you this morning? I was sleeping and when I woke up you were gone."

"I know. I was starving, I left you an order of roast pork and white rice in the fridge."

"You did? I thought that was Grandma shit. Where you about to head with all them Dutches, Smokey?"

"I'm about to go to my people's crib, then we going to make it happen."

She then asked me for twenty dollars. I told her to take it out of my stash and I'll see her later. I saw cabbie, and we walked away from each other. I got in the cab and told cabbie the address and to put the music on.

Cabbie was at the green light, but it turned yellow, then red, so we were stuck at the light. Myquan was lookin' out his window, staring at Sandra and Sandra was staring back at him.

Look at these two motherfuckers!!! I can't believe it! They are creeping. Myquan is a snake and a molester. Sandra ain't but one year older than me. He is crazy. He is 27-years-old. If her family knew about this, Myquan would get fucked up. Especially her brother Pook—he would knock Myquan the fuck out. He is mad, sneaky, and when the shit hits the fan I don't wanna have anything to do with that.

Myquan must have been in her car to get Sandra's attentions, 'cause she don't even be around like that. That's crazy, 'cause Trina, his girlfriend, lives next door and she and her cousins are my home girls. I fucks with them hard body and they brother Ninja and they cousin Hasan. Matter of fact, Ninja got a bad crush on Sandra and be beating and extorting Myquan every chance he gets, 'cause Myquan be fighting with his sister . . .

I was madder than a motherfucker and didn't know why. I had some type of feelings for Sandra but didn't understand them, and now I had a hate streak for Myquan for stealing what was mine from me.

What is wrong with Sandra? Do she not know I have a thing for her? How could she know? That's a secret I keep to myself, but how could she mess with people I get money with and messing with girls' men that I am cool with? How do I look smiling and eating and smoking in Trina and Em' crib when my home girl is fucking her man? When shit comes to a head I could see now that I'm gonna be in the middle of a hot mess and gonna have to smooth things out. Anyway, until the dark comes to light I'm just gonna play stupid. I got my own issues to deal with.

"Yo cabbie how much longer?"

(11)

I arrived at Nubush's house and she was waiting outside of it for me. I got out the cab and told cabbie the same thing I always tell him, "I'll call you when I'm ready to leave." Damn! This girl was good looking. Her skin was a caramel complexion, almond shaped eyes, a pretty smile, a nice curvaceous body that stood on bowed legs. Uhm! She was bad.

"You look nice, Deidra, you changed your clothes."

"Yeah, didn't want you to think I was a Hoodlum."

"Don't worry, when I saw you that was the last thing I thought," she said while I walked into her house.

"What's all that in the bag?"

"My meditation medicine, you smoke?"

"Nah, and you gonna have to smoke that outside. I got a way to smoke and it doesn't go through the house."   ✎

The Birth

Denise Irby

 Denise wrote this story at a time when almost all of the girls who attended her workshop each week were incarcerated mothers like herself. During her incarceration, the story was shared among juvenile justice reform advocates, first in Harlem at a reading organized by New York State's Coalition for Women Prisoners, and later at the 14th Annual Conference: Prepared and Proactive—Laws, Policies and Practices in Youth Violence and Gang Prevention, which took place on November 17, 2011 at Hofstra University. Denise grew up in Manhasset, NY and currently resides in West Hempstead, where she is now raising her daughter. She enjoys reading and writing and playing sports. Her goals for life are to raise her daughter, giving her the life she never had, and going back to school to become the veterinarian she's always wanted to be. Poignantly, she illuminates the conditions of incarcerated teens forced to give birth in conditions that most of us cannot even imagine.

"**W**hat time is it?"
"6:35."
"What time is it?"
"6:40."
"What time is it?"
"6:45."

It's Thursday, June 9, 2011. Here I am at Nassau County correctional facility, nine months pregnant, 2 cm dilated and four days away from my due date.

"Why do you keep asking the time?" Kera asks me.

"Because I think I'm having contractions."

"What do you mean you THINK?!" She says with emphasis on the "think."

"I'm feeling pressure and tightness, it goes away and then comes back, I'm tryna time it."

"Well you keep asking the time every 5 minutes, yes its contractions."

"Oh," I say.

Next thing I know the whole dorm starts going crazy.

"She's going into labor! The baby's coming. Officer! Officer! It's time!" the inmates are screaming.

"I gotta go to the bathroom," I say nonchalantly as if nothing's going on.

"No, no, no, you have to sit; you're not suppose to use the bathroom."

"I gotta get in the shower," I say heading for my cell.

"No, you have to sit."

"Well I gotta get my shirt and ID," I say getting up from the chair.

"No, I will get it," Mrs. Pat says.

"Can you grab me a bag of chips while you're at it?"

"No! You can't eat anything."

Great! I think to myself. I have to pee, I'm hungry as hell, I want to shower, and apparently I'm not allowed to do anything but sit and wait, wait and sit.

"I'ma call your mom and Justin and let them know you're going into labor."

Unfortunately, neither of them will be allowed to see me or be in the delivery room for the birth. In fact, I won't be allowed to contact anyone till after the baby is born.

"Irby, don't have the baby yet, medical is on the way," the officer says over the loud speaker. The entire dorm starts laughing.

"The baby gonna be here before medical," Mrs. Pat jokes.

"Fuck a bullshit medical. I need an ambulance," I say.

15 minutes passes by before medical comes running into the dorm, asking stupid questions such as "What's going on, how are you feeling, and are you okay?" I'm wanting to slap the living shit outta them.

I remain calm, answering "I'm going into labor, and yes, I'm okay."

Duh is the only thing I can think.

After repeatedly telling the nurses that the contractions are five minutes apart and having my vitals taken, I am wheeled down to medical. There I am faced with the stupidest questions I have ever been asked.

"How far along are you?"

It takes all my might not to yell back, "Obviously if I'm going into labor I'm full term!"

I just simply say, "I'm nine months, I'm due June 13th."

"Oh my God! Are you sure you're that far along?"

Obviously, you dumb ass, I think to myself. This new medical shit is pathetic.

I didn't get to the hospital until after eight dealing with these simple motherfuckers. By then my contractions were three minutes apart. After being rushed through the hospital hallways, handcuffed, escorted by two officers and the public looking on, I was hooked up to some machine that monitored my contractions as well as the baby's heartbeat. I was bum-rushed with more questions and papers needing my signature.

After answering the questions, signing the papers, and two hours later the doctor approaches me.

"Ms. Irby we are gonna need you to walk around for a while to induce your labor."

"Um, okay," I reply. At the moment I feel something wet.

"Um, excuse me," I say. "I'm leaking and I don't know what it is."

The doctor comes over to me, sticks two fingers inside, then says to the nurse, "Her membrane has been ruptured. She's about 30% . . . wait . . . yea, 30 over 100." She pulls out and I see the blood-covered glove.

"What does that mean?" I ask nervously, scared to hear the answer.

"It means that your water broke and you're about 3 cm dilated."

"What about the blood, is that normal?" I ask immediately.

"Yes, everything is just fine," she assures me. "I guess you really didn't want to walk!" she says jokingly.

I laugh. Truth is she was right. I wasn't looking forward to walking around the maternity ward handcuffed and shackled, I guess

Kylie wasn't either. They move me to my own room where they continued to monitor me.

"Would you like an epidural?" the nurse asks.

"No, not right now. I'm not feeling any pain," I say with my eyes glued to the TV. I was watching the Heat vs. Mavericks finals game four, of course going for Miami. In the middle of the third quarter, with Miami in the lead, it hit me. The excruciating pain was unbearable.

"Oh nurse, I would like the epidural now," I say, holding onto the bedrail, ready to tear it off.

"She's 50 over 100," the doctor says sticking her fingers inside me.

After another 20 minutes and four pain-filled contractions, I finally get the epidural. I slowly start to nod off, only to be awakened by loud beeping noises. Nurses start running into the room, checking the monitor. I'm startled.

"What's going on?" I ask.

"The baby's heart rate is dropping."

Now I'm intent. Looking at the monitor I see the numbers slowly dropping down from 100 to 90 to 80.

"Lay on your right side," the nurses tell me, so I comply.

"Switch to your left," she says again, so I do so,

"Is she okay?"

"Yes," she replies, as she watches the numbers on the monitor start to go back up. I drift off to sleep, only to be awakened by loud beeping noises. I'm alert, immediately fearing for my baby girl. The nurses come pouring back into the room. I see the numbers on the screen dropping again.

"Is she OK?" I ask nervously.

The doctor sticks her fingers inside, wiggles them and then tells me to lay on my left side. The numbers slowly start to increase again. The nurses leave and I'm off to sleep, only to be awakened by the loud beeping noises once again. The nurses return.

"It's happening again?" I say to the nurse.

"Yes," she says back to me.

"That's bad, isn't it?" I say commenting and asking at the same time.

"It's not healthy for the baby," she says. "This is the third time this has happened, a baby's heart rate isn't supposed to drop no lower than 100. It could be very critical for the baby if it does."

I look at the monitor—it displays 76. I start to panic.

"We have one more option, but if this happens again we would have to prepare you for a C-section," she tells me, and then tells another nurse to please bring her amniotic fluid. At that point I start to beg God and my baby girl.

"What is that for?" I ask curiously.

"It's amniotic fluids. It's gonna help the baby feel more comfortable being that there's no more fluid inside you. She's being squished by the contacting muscles, which is causing her a little stress . . . this should help."

"Is that why her heart rate keeps dropping?" I ask.

"Yes, that, and mostly because she won't move, she's very lazy, it seems as if she's going to sleep."

"I see you're taking after your momma already," I say to my stomach.

I laugh, so does the officer. The officer. I almost forgot she was here. A silence comes over me. I closed my eyes and lay quietly in the bed, as if I was sleeping, but I wasn't. All I could think about was how my boyfriend wasn't here. I won't be holding his hand during the delivery. He won't be here for the birth of our princess, his first child—no cutting the umbilical cord, no holding her. How could I hurt him this way? Because of me he couldn't take part in the birth of his first child, because of me he couldn't cut the umbilical cord of his baby girl, because of me he couldn't hold her, he couldn't be there the way he wanted to, everything he was looking forward to doing he couldn't, because of me. It was my fault. I felt like shit. It wasn't fair to him, he didn't have a say in it. I felt like dying.

The doctor walks in and snaps me outta my thoughts.

"Push" she says. I give it my all. "Push" she says. I go at it again.

"You have to push!" she says again.

"I am."

"No you're not," she says.

"I'm not? I thought I was."

We all laugh as I try again.

"There you go," she says, "now you're pushing."

They start to push me to the delivery room with the officer following.

I push. She counts to ten. I stop.

"She's coming!" I hear her yell, "keep pushing." I do. She counts to ten. I stop.

"Ok, one more time."

I push. Out comes the baby.

"6:43 A.M., it's a girl," the doctor announces. I hear her cry. My eyes tear up.

"You did a good job, she's beautiful," I hear a voice say. I look up and all I see is blue and gray. It's the officer.

"Thanks," I say softly, wishing to myself that it was Justin's voice I was hearing.

I hold her for the first time, my child, my baby girl, my daughter and then it hits me; I'm a mother now. I glance down at her, "Kylie Nicole-Lynn Thurmond," I whisper to her. She smiles. I thank God for such a beautiful gift. They take me back to my room, shortly after Kylie returns. I hold her. I feed her. I burp her. I can't put her down or take my eyes off her. I'm amazed by her beauty. She's precious. Delicate like a flower or an angel. My flower. My angel.

I whisper sweet nothings in her ear. "Mommy loves you, your Daddy loves you, sorry Daddy couldn't be here; you're so beautiful, so precious."

I see her smile, I smile. She opens her eyes, it's like I'm staring back at my own. She's so innocent.

Her father arrives, but he's not allowed to see me. Being that I'm still in the custody of the jail, he must follow the jail's visiting hours and has to check in with the jail first. He spends time at the nursery with Kylie and tells me he will be back later because he left his ID at home, rushing out the door to get to the hospital. The officers tell him the last visit is at 7 P.M.

My parents make it to the hospital around 6:30.

"Whose little Chinese baby is that?" my mom jokes immediately taking the baby out of my arms.

"You sure you wasn't with a Chinese man?" my dad continues.

"I'm sure," I say laughing.

I look at my parents taking turns kissing and holding their grandchild. For my dad it's his fifth, for my mom, her first. I can see the excitement in her eyes. Kylie is quiet. They stay for an hour and then leave.

My boyfriend comes back—it's ten after seven. He tells me that he can't stay.

"Why?" I ask him.

"They say I got back too late."

"What time did you get here?"

"Five to seven, but they said I had to be here before 6:45 to make the last visit." He kisses me and then Kylie.

"I love you both," he says and then disappears.

I call him later and he tells me that he will visit me on Monday since there's no visits for the jail on weekends, but he is definitely coming to see his daughter first thing tomorrow. We sit on the phone for hours.

"I can't wait to have both of my girls at home and in my arms."

"I know . . . I can't either."

"Let me speak to the babz."

I put the phone to her ear. I think back to how he used to talk to my stomach, and how I used to put the phone to my stomach so he could talk to her when we was apart. I can't wait until all three of us is together as a family.

I continued to talk to Justin, watch TV, feed, change, and hold Kylie. The next three days were the exact same.

Sunday comes around, and now I must do the hardest thing I've ever had to do. Today is the day that me and Kylie have to go our separate ways.

"Normally we discharge at 9 A.M., but because of your circumstances you will be discharged at a later time," the nurse informs me. I'm thankful for the extra hours. I spend the whole day apologizing to her.

"I'm sorry, Babz. Mommy loves you. You mean the world to me. You're my everything. Don't you ever forget that, don't forget about me," I say repeatedly into her ear.

For the remainder of the day I talk on the phone with Justin, watching Kylie. Watching her smile, watching her open her eyes, watching her sleep. She looks like him. Cheeks, nose and ears—they're all his.

"You're my heart," I say to her. The time is drawing near and reality is starting to hit me. It's 6 P.M. I call Justin crying.

"Mama, what's wrong?"

"It's almost time."

"Don't worry, baby. Everything is okay. She's gonna be fine. Just try to stay strong for her."

"I'm trying but I can't, I need you, Daddy."

"Babe, just stay calm. Talk to me."

We continue to talk until 6:45.

"Babe, I gotta go now."

"No, please don't hang up!" I beg him

"I have to so I can meet your mom at her house when she gets back with Babz."

"Okay," I sniffle. Two minutes later the nurse comes into the room.

"I have to get the baby ready to go. Your mother is here," she says.

I look at the clock. It's 6:50. I have ten minutes. It's just like my mother to be early. The tears start to fall from my eyes and onto Kylie as I say my final goodbyes. When she takes Kylie from my arms I break down. My tears fall down like rain. There's nothing in the world that's more painful than a child being taken from its mother's arms. That's just another dagger in my heart. I'm crying uncontrollably. After about ten minutes of crying nonstop the officer walks in.

"I'ma allow your mother to come in, two minutes and no touching." I don't respond, just keep crying.

"Niecy . . ." I hear a shaky voice say my name. I turn around to see my mother. She's crying too. My tears fall even harder.

"Don't worry, honey, you know she's in good hands," I hear her say.

"I know but it's too hard, I don't wanna let her go." I cry back. I think to myself if this is how my mother felt when she had to give me up. I wonder if this reminds her of that day. I look at her; I can tell in her eyes that it does.

"Thank you," I say.

"Anytime," she replies.

I never imagined I would be like my mother. I always told myself I never would. First, my mother having to give me up and go to a drug program, and then me having to give my daughter up to return to jail.

"I'm a bad mother," I whisper to myself and continue to cry.

"You Were Such a Beautiful Woman..."

Taylor Nolte

As with many women who come to our workshop in the jail, Taylor came to her writing with the question, "How did I get here?" Certainly she had been doing her very best, shouldering responsibilities that would have been daunting to most adults. Shouldering way too much for a 17-year-old until, in the blink of an eye, in a moment of bad choice to drive while drinking, her entire life changed. In spite of this serious interruption of her life plan to join the Marines, in a circumstance where many others of her age would have caved in to bitterness, Taylor always presented herself with a calm abiding maturity and acceptance, taking responsibility for her mistakes, and intent on making the best of her "time." (While serving her sentence in prison she is a full-time straight-A college student).

In sharing this writing, her one concern was that her anger towards her mother at the time we meet her on the page would be misinterpreted as a lack of love and respect, when in fact it came out of the fearful and desperate heart of a young and very devoted, struggling daughter. Though shy to share this piece, it is her hope that it might comfort others in the same, all too common predicament of living with an addicted parent.

I pulled into my driveway and laid my head back on the seat with a sigh. This was the seventh day in a row working at the pizza place. *Sixty hours this week,* I thought, *more days, more hours, more money. Whatever pays the bills* . . . I realized I had only ten minutes to get ready for night school. Damn, I had to hurry. I walked to the door thinking, I hope Mommy cleaned up. I walked through the sliding doors into the living room, immediately disgusted as usual.

Cigarette smoke filled the air. My mom's bed, the couch, was a mess as she sat there in the same clothes she'd had on for the last three days—her boyfriend's sweat pants and a shirt. She used a kitchen chair in the living room as a table with a filled ashtray, her drink and more junk on it.

On the floor lay more cigarette butts and the half-gallon of vodka, half empty, with her Diet Pepsi next to it. I knew her back-up was in the freezer. What a hot mess. Her drink in her hand was almost done . . . soon she'd refill. I took all this in in an instant as soon as I walked in. Certainly not the mother I used to come home to. That mother had burgundy big 80s hair, green eyes and red lipstick. That mother made me breakfast in bed and put a scoop of ice cream in my hot cocoa. She taught me how to do my make-up and tease my hair. This woman in my living room—her hair was brittle and frizzy, her lips were bare and chapped, and freckles covered her face.

"Poo-poo head, bring me to the store."

Ugg, I hated when she called me that.

"Wait till I get ready for school and I'll see if I have time." I looked at the clock . . . damn, five minutes left. I poked my head in Grandma's room.

"Hey, Grandma, are you hungry?"

"No thanks, baby girl, I just ate some oatmeal."

"Are you sure? I'm leaving for school soon."

My Grandma was my world. She was an overweight eighty-year-old woman who always wore dresses. Her eyes were hazel and she smelled like Elizabeth Taylor's White Diamonds. I noticed her hair was growing—I had to cut it soon. She too was changing in front of my eyes, becoming weaker in the knees. She used her walker to get up from her desk and transfer to her hover-round wheelchair. Me and Mommy called it her motorcycle. She started it up and zoomed right past me.

I got dressed for school, still smelling like bread from work. No time to shower . . . damn.

"Okay, I'm ready."

"Let's go," my mom said.

"Um . . . I don't have time. I can't be late for school. Take Grandma's car."

"I don't like driving that car. Plus, you know I had a drink."

Yeah . . . a drink, I thought. I closed out the rest of the argument. I'd become very good at practicing selective hearing and tuning out the slur in her words.

Coming home from school was no better than coming home from work. As I walked in the door, I heard Mommy screaming at Grandma. Oh Jesus, not again!

"You're a horrible mother . . . you always were! That's why Daddy died. You know, he cheated on you!" my mom yelled viciously at my Grandma.

"Just leave me alone!" Grandma cried back.

I could see her getting upset and hearing my mother talk to her like that stabbed me like a dull knife. I had to break in.

"You're the horrible mother! You're always drunk while I bust my ass for the both of you!"

I had to defend Grandma because I know she didn't start it.

"Grandma, go relax and listen to music."

I turned to my mother, "What are you doing? How dare you speak to Grandma like that! Who do you think you are? Clean this living room . . . it's a fucking mess!"

I knew their fight was about my mother stealing Grandma's money, like always. I opened the freezer and took her vodka and ran to the toilet.

"I hate this shit . . . it's the fucking Devil!" I yelled.

"Taylor don't!"

I poured it out before she got to me. She pushed me.

"That costs money! What do you think you're doing you little bitch!"

"Yeah . . . Grandma's money!"

She would do anything to get her alcohol . . . lie, steal money, or even ask my friends to take her to the liquor store since I refused to enable her. It was so embarrassing.

I had to get out of there. I had to get away. I left to go meet my friends outside. Hanging out with them was my escape. With them

I could act my age, have conversations like what we'd do with a million dollars, or what would happen if the world really did come to an end in 2012. I met up with my homies and we played badminton in my yard for a couple of hours. As the night came to an end, we said our goodbyes and I watched them pull out of my driveway. I sat on a patio chair and smoked a cigarette, drinking the rest of my drink and watching the television flicker through the blinds.

I knew my mother was in there holding her drink in her hand. It was the same as holding a knife in her hand, because she was killing herself with that poison. She was moving less and less from the couch each day. Something in my gut had me frightened. This time, instead of worrying about the bills, or school, or her getting a job, I feared for her life. I'd seen my uncle die from alcoholism. When you drink like she was drinking there was no happy ending. Maybe she didn't help with anything in my life or Grandma's, but she was still my mother, regardless of what this disease had turned her into.

I finished the rest of my drink and debated whether to sleep in my car or pop a DVD in my TV. Guilt and sorrow were pumping through my veins. I hated seeing her in her own filth, looking like hell, drinking around the clock. This was not the life of a happy woman. How did she get to this rock-bottom level of depression and loneliness? I needed to do something even though I always ended up feeling helpless. I was sick and tired of making plans with her to go job hunting, buying her an outfit, just to get turned down the next day because she was "sick." She's always sick. But who the hell prescribed her vodka? I tried to hold the tears back and decided I was going to go inside.

I walked in and she was sitting on the couch with her cigarette and her drink. I tried to walk past her and say goodnight, but I couldn't. No matter how hard I tried the sobbing came out and I couldn't stop. I gave her a hug and she hugged me back. I let go and sat on the chair across from her. I had to do something and this time I wasn't taking no for an answer. I couldn't let her die like this.

"Mommy, why do you keep doing this? Can't you see you're killing yourself? I know you're not happy and I'm sorry, Mommy, but you can't do this to me and Grandma. Stop being selfish!"

She couldn't understand my blubbering cries, so I tried to calm down and repeated what I had just said.

"This is what not working has done to me," she said.

"So, let's get you a job. I'll take you shopping and buy you a new wardrobe."

I stared at my mother, knowing she couldn't work in the condition she was in. Bartending was out because she was way too slow, she moved like a turtle and acted like she was eighty but she was only forty.

"You were such a beautiful woman . . . You still are, but you don't care about anything anymore. Listen, if Chris doesn't treat you right, let's go and get you a new man. Once you work and get out and have your own money, you'll be back to the same cocky woman you were."

She played with the straw in her drink, swirling it in a circular motion around the melting ice.

"I just need to work. I'm a social person . . . I need to be around people. That's why I loved my job . . . Bartending, it's what I do. You like to do what you love for work."

I got a glimpse of how she felt inside . . . a scared, lonely little girl who felt incompetent in doing something new.

"Mommy, sometimes you have to do what you have to do. Almost any job you socialize with people. You'll feel so much better getting out there again, looking beautiful, and breaking necks . . ." I said trying to boost her confidence.

"Mom, you're killing yourself with this alcohol. It's not making anything better. Didn't you learn from Uncle Kevin? You can't go that route, Mommy. You have to stop! You wake up and drink 24/7 . . . that's not normal."

"Don't you notice I've calmed down? I told Chris I want to check out an AA meeting . . ."

Denial! I felt like I was running in circles with her.

"You keep putting me down," she whined, "and I don't want to get up. I have to want to do it. You can't make me!" She paused and looked into her glass. "Honey, go get me some ice, would you?"

I ignored her and walked into my room. How could she just brush this off? I felt robbed of my mother and robbed of my childhood. She didn't care anymore. Coming home to argue with her and to clean up her mess was becoming overwhelming.

Another night of crying myself to sleep.

"Beep . . . beep . . . beep!" I hated the noise of my alarm clock. I had an appointment to check out this studio apartment that I'd been thinking about moving to, but I called and cancelled. How am I going to leave these two people who need me so much? My mother would eat Grandma alive and spit her out. I had a feeling that once I did move out I wouldn't see them again . . . especially my mother. These would be my last moments with them and I wasn't ready for that. I needed them like they needed me.

My mother surprised me by coming into my room with breakfast. She made me an egg-in-a-nest and a chocolate milk shake with some soda. She sat on my bed and handed me the plate. Breakfast in bed? Today really was going to be a good day! I loved when she did these things. My mother was still here, but seldom seen—like an eclipse.

I told her I wasn't leaving, that we'd stay together.

Heading westbound on the LIE wasn't as exciting as eastbound. The sky was getting darker, reflecting my mood. Exit 51, the one I took for work, came faster than I wanted . . . back into the routine. School was getting more intense as the year came to an end.

At home, it was like me and Mommy hardly talked. Grandma told me she wasn't eating very much. I tried to call a few of my mom's friends and family members to try to arrange an intervention but no one seemed to care. I didn't know what to do but keep my life movin'. I felt like she'd started getting worse quick.

Monday came and I presented my mother with flowers and one of those jumbo cards. She actually looked happy. It felt good to put a smile on her face.

The due date for my Health Project was about a week later. It was a serious percentage of my grade and included a seven-page essay, a presentation with a visual. I had to do a good job to maintain my good streak of 90s. That night, I got home from school and the lights were off as usual and Mom was asleep on the couch. I hopped onto the computer to get busy. A few hours later I heard my mom scream from the living room, "Madeline! Madeline!"

What the hell? I thought. It's nearly 4 A.M. She's probably having a crazy dream.

"She's been actin' real strange tonight, Taylor," I heard my Grandma mutter.

"What do you mean?" I became really scared and stood up from my desk when I heard my mother call for Madeline again.

"Mom??" I was surprised to see her eyes open. She had crazy eyes, like there was nobody behind them.

"Where'd Madeline go? Tell her I forgot something!"

"What the hell are you talking about!? Madeline was never here! Are you dreaming?" I suddenly grew very angry, feeling like why is she doing this shit now?

Earlier in the day I'd hidden her vodka from her. I'm surprised she ain't fiending.

Curtains separating desperate families. Doctors and nurses running frantic. The smell of anesthetic and the sound of shoes clicking on the linoleum floors. The beeping of the machines. I stood next to my mother holding her hand. She looked even worse under the fluorescent lighting. She was so yellow, so weak. She asked me to take a picture so she could see what she looked like. "I'll never drink again!" she managed to blurt out.

It was only me and her, with the occasional nurse poking in. "She's dehydrated," I said to the nurse. "She needs water!"

"I'm sorry, she can't drink. The IVs are hydrating her."

My mother's tongue looked like the tongue of a cat. Finally the nurse gave me wet Q-tips.

"What the hell am I supposed to do with these? Where's the fucking doctor? She needs attention now!"

The nurse demonstrated how to wet the inside of her mouth with the Q-tip to keep it from drying out and then left.

Where was anybody to help? I thought. I couldn't believe Grandma was home alone and I wondered what she must be feeling, waiting to hear from us. But it was just me and Mommy in our little cubicle of hell. It felt like everything around me was in slow motion. People screaming, bleeding, clipboards being passed around everywhere. A social worker came to speak to me, but I blew her off and went outside. Walking past each curtain, seeing the patients with their families. I turned around. Mommy was alone, but sleeping now.

Outside, the weather was beautiful but my mood remained the same. I reached into my purse for my cigarettes. Shit! I didn't have any. Everything had happened so quickly, I'd left them at home when the ambulance came. I leaned against the wall of the building and slid to the ground. My legs couldn't hold me up anymore. I felt like I couldn't handle this anymore by myself. I kept screaming, "It's over! It's over!" and cried harder than I'd ever cried in my life. I knew this day was coming and now my mother was here in Good Sam and she was going to die!

I kept hiccupping, gasping for air, my whole body shaking. I rocked aback and forth. It was hard to be optimistic when it's the truth. Just the other day we were watching *Desperate Housewives* together. Just the other week we were at each other's throats with vicious words. How did this happen? How did this happen so fast? She's not getting out! She's not getting out!

My phone rang but I didn't want to talk to anyone right now. My emotions had me by my throat and I was suffocating. This is my mother—the person who gave birth to me and has been there for me for most of my life! She's in trouble and pain . . . internal bleeding and dehydration, liver and kidney failure and getting a blood transfusion. How could her body just fall apart so quickly? Why didn't I notice this? I should have been home more! It's my fault! She was my responsibility! What did I do wrong?   ✎

"I Just Wanted a New Gift..."

Jodie Biondo

While on the surface, Jodie's background is very different from that of the other young women in this anthology— adoption at the age of five by a female couple who provide her a rich, caring childhood in London and become her two mothers—once she started to write, gathering strength from the stories of the other young women whose backgrounds more closely echoed her own early memories, she was able to call onto the page those first ghosts of her past.

So often the process of writing together, whether in jail or on the outside, creates commonalities across those barriers of race, class and culture that keep us apart, as our ghosts "talk to one another" through the words that bubble to the surface, and we discover that we are not all that different.

The numbness, the relief, the high. It had all faded. A flash of lightning—there one minute, then gone forever. I saw black with a slight light in the distance. My body so numb—nothing I had ever felt before. It was peace at last and no one could take it away. I couldn't reach the distance, the numbness was fading, and the pain was reoccurring. It was worse than living, it was survival.

I strained to open my eyes. I saw blurred figures running around me, muffled sounds repeating the same five words I didn't want to hear. My mind was racing. I couldn't connect with any physical pain. I felt paralyzed. The mental pain was excruciating, knowing that I was still alive. The silence, the relief, the peace flashed before me and in a matter of seconds it was all gone.

Growing up, our parents give us many gifts, but the best gift we are given is the gift of life. Without that one sperm, which traveled and raced hundreds of others in order to reach that one egg and fertilize it to create me, I wouldn't be alive today. It seemed like such a long and tiring process. Was it really worth it? All the time and energy put in when it could be taken away in the blink of an eye.

The first three years growing up I didn't connect to my mother. Yes, she gave birth to me, but every time she looked at me she had this blank look on her face, like she didn't care. I had spent nine long months connected inside her womb. I was a piece of her and it was like she was angry with me for being here. She gave me the best gift but didn't care to build me up and teach me how to use it.

I lay there with wires and tubes all over my body—that annoying beeping sound, its repetition running concurrent with my heart beat. I opened my eyes to see the same walls, hear the same noises, and feel the same feeling. It was like I was born again, except this time I knew what life was. Yes, it's a gift, but if it's given at the wrong time, then there is no point in giving it at all. As I lay there and observed my surroundings, I realized that I hated this gift. It wasn't fun. It wasn't like anyone else's. It sucked. My thoughts were racing and even though I felt nothing, I knew the feeling was there. Why did I pull through? Why was I still alive? I just wanted a new gift, one that wasn't broken and torn and so difficult to put back together. I felt the tears trickling down my face, my body tensing. I closed my eyes and drifted away.

It was April 4, 1998. I was six years old. I was so excited I could hardly stay still. Today was the day my new family was coming to pick me up. It was a brisk spring morning. I had put on my favorite flowered dress. It was white with a lace trim and had pink and purple flowers all over. I slid into my new white tights and snapped the buckles to my best white shoes. I was rushing all around my room, gathering every last thing before they arrived. As the time of their arrival drew closer, I sat on the couch staring out the window. I couldn't believe today was the day.

I had met these two women many times. They had taken me to see movies, we ate at beautiful restaurants, and we played together in the park. They were perfect for me. They also had a piece of me— my sister. She was four years older than me and had been adopted one year prior. I felt safe and close with her. She was my source of love during my first years of development. I felt a deep connection to her and I knew that if she was happy with these new "moms" I would be too.

I was so ecstatic words couldn't begin to describe the butterflies in my stomach and the warmth in my heart. There was no more waiting and disappointment. Today I was no longer a little blond-haired blue-eyed orphan. Today I received the best gift. Not only did I get one new mommy, I got two! Today was my fairytale dream come true.

A black Ford Fiesta pulled up. My stomach was in a knot and I felt tingling sensations throughout my body. I wanted someone to pinch me and tell me it was really happening. I couldn't believe it. I jumped up as I saw my new moms and my sister walking up the path to the front door. I opened the door before they could even knock and greeted them. My sister was wearing black Adidas track suit bottoms, a green Nike T-shirt and brand new Nike sneakers.

She was smiling at me and said, "Hey Sis, are you all ready to come and live with us in London?"

I answered so quickly, "Yes."

My new mothers came into my foster home and met with my caretakers and social worker, whilst I showed my sister where all my things were packed and ready. We put all my things in the boot of the little Fiesta and came inside. My moms were standing in the hallway. They asked me if I was ready. My face lit up like a Christmas tree and I grabbed my little purse and said, "Yes, let's go!"

The constant beeping awoke me and I opened my eyes. I had to open and close them a few times before I could see clearly. I felt a warm hand enclosed in my cold shaky hand and I looked over to see both my moms staring back at me, with tears in their eyes, their faces pale and eyelids drooping from lack of sleep. They smiled at me and told me they weren't going to leave me. One of my mothers kissed my forehead and wrapped her arms around me and just held me. I felt her warmth running through my veins, her smell overpowering my senses. I felt so safe, like nothing could harm me, she just gave me protection and I knew it was going to be okay.

I looked up and saw the women who chose me, who did nothing but love and cherish me, gave me everything I needed, wanted and desired. But as I looked up at them, they were tired, worn and sad. They did everything in their power to make me happy and I showed no thanks. I didn't listen, I drank, I smoked and I disrespected them.

Why were they still here sitting at the edge of my bed, nurturing me and caring for me when I had hurt them deeply? I felt the pain weighing me down, my thoughts circling my brain. I couldn't live with it, I'd be better off alone, they would be better off without me. I couldn't bear to look up any longer.

The Dad That I Love and Honor

Daytona Goodwin

Daytona joined the Voices writing workshop in September of 2011 and worked with the group until her move upstate in June of this year. From the onset, Day-Day, as she preferred to be called, said she wrote because she was angry. In her natural poet's voice, she wrote furiously about her anger and missteps, her recurring dreams and longing for genuine understanding and caring. Perhaps Day-Day's greatest challenge was moving from her innate verses and spoken word style to fuller scenes and storylines, to weaving more concrete images and moments of being along with the metaphors running through her unique rhythm and rhyme. This brave and honest letter in particular—a letter to her father— was the last piece she shared in the workshop, and captures this growth as a writer. What distinguishes this letter as more than just a trite "letter to your parent" exercise is the layering of story that emerges in reaching out to her father to say how she truly feels about him. As a literary device, the letter captures Day-Day not only writing it, but her father also receiving her words in jail, the letter itself a living piece of her story.

Dear Dad,

I made it. I hope you're very proud, I'm sure you will be. I'm not losin' n-e sleep. I eat every day now. Fightin', I slowed down a lot. I show everyone respect, and honestly, it sucks to say, but I also think of you. I wonder, do you miss me or even think of me? Do you wonder what I have become in life? Wait, how 'bout how many kids I have? Do you wonder did me and my mom receive your gift? I doubt it.

Why did you leave? Was it because you were scared? If so, what the fuck were you scared of? If you could do it all over again, would you make up for lost time or would you repeat this fucked-up episode. What about my brothers and sisters? Did you ever think that I would like to meet them? How about your funeral? Do you want me to show up? Do you even think, what if I was your killer one day?

Well, let me tell you about my moms. She's so sorry that she even met you. She hates when I ask about your no-good-tired-ass. If you wanted to, she wouldn't give you the time and the day to apologize. By the way, she made it all on her own. She didn't need you and neither did I. She raised three boys and one girl. My birthday passed. I'm grown now. Now she's raisin' another girl. She just turned one in July. Sometime I wonder what she thinks about her mom and dad. But at least her dad and mom do come around time to time.

N-E-ways, like I said, she raised us well. So well you couldn't even tell we didn't have our father in our life. So to this day she is our mother and father and she's more of a father then you will ever be. Oh, by the way, she's legally blind. Her eyes cocked out on her when I was 13, and she still made it. Just thought I'd tell you that.

Well, me, like I said, I made it and I'm not talking 'bout successfully. I made it in your footsteps—started smokin' weed at nine, poppin' pills since 14 and started jailin' since 15. Caught my first five and a half year bid like you. Date bitches just like you. I never had a boyfriend, but I don't know 'bout you. I don't have kids like you. Oh, and I was born negative. Me or my mom didn't receive your little gift called AIDS, so I can say we Guccii. Sucks to be you. I wanted to come find your pussy ass to see if you had answers to my questions but that's out, 'cause now I'm facin' ten years in prison. When I come home, I'll be 32. You'll probably be gone. Maybe not. Who knows? Well, just know I hate you. Well, not hate, but dislike you for the dead beat you turned out to be. But I love and honor you for giving me life, 'cause I turned out to be the best thing you never had.

Always with feelings,
Daytona Goodwin

110 Degrees

Esperanza Caminante

 *While from our earliest school years we study and celebrate the stories of children who endured great hardship and showed great bravery as they crossed over to a new land or blazed new frontiers, with current attitudes to border crossings we do not listen enough to the voices of the immigrant children of today who were asked to rise to heroic acts beyond their young years. From the moment Esperaza was given the tools she would need to craft a compelling "Page One Moment," she held her writing group spellbound as she added scene upon scene every week. Because we never ask the women in our writing groups what brought them to jail, we have no idea what transpired between the end of this story and the time of Esperanza's arrest, nor what sentence snatched her from the jail where she was starting to open up as the details you will read here came back to her. We can only admire the fortitude and spirit of this young girl, as we ask our readers to think more deeply about what it means to create such fences, barriers, and obstacles that children, separated from their families, never choosing the journeys they are sent on, must struggle to surmount.*

It's around 110 degrees; it is so hot, so humid, I'm sweating, the air is dry and it's hard to breathe. I know I'm not in the desert, but it almost feels like it. I can't stand the heat and the sun.

This is Mexico D.F. (Mexico City) and I'm waiting on the streets.

I really don't know who is coming for us. I know my destination, but I have no idea what's going to happen from this point on. In a way I'm excited. I get to see new places. It's a new adventure and I feel free like an adult.

I hear a car and the noisy sound of the brakes against the rotor.

I can smell the burning brakes in the air. I notice a black SUV with tinted windows. The street is empty. The doors open, the driver remains inside, and every other man gets out— around five men. They are all wearing black T-shirts, black cargo pants, black boots, and their faces are covered with a black bandana all the way from their noses to their chins. I notice how two of them have golden chains with crosses around their necks.

A man is screaming. As soon as he steps out of the SUV, he gives us the order to get inside, "Get in. Hurry up—NOW!"

I've never seen them before in my life. I don't know any of them. What is going on?

As soon as I step inside the SUV, I feel the air conditioning hit my skin. It feels cold and nice inside the SUV. I am able to smell a mix of antifreeze, cologne and cigarettes.

Everything has turned dark. I cannot see anything. My hearing becomes twice as acute. As I'm touching and feeling the texture of the fabric covering my face, the voice of a man is saying, "Don't try to take it off. It is for your own protection."

They put hoods on our heads to avoid our seeing where we are or where we are going. I brush my arm against somebody else by my side. I know this person very well. I know the way she smells. I know every single thing about her. A relief invades my body. My heartbeat gets back to normal. I'm okay now, my sister still by my side. She is still with me.

I don't know what time it is. I can't tell where we are. The only thing I know is I'm still inside the SUV and its engine keeps on going.

I fell asleep. I guess I was tired. My sister—I recognize her voice—she is talking to me, trying to wake me up. My hood is off.

As the doors open, I clearly see the blue sky, the white fluffy clouds, and the nice sunny day. Outside men are waiting for us. They quickly say to us to hurry up and get inside the house.

I'm very good at observing my surroundings. It does not look like a nice neighborhood, a lot of movement going on in the streets, lots of people. It's loud and hot. The house looks like a cute little and colorful cottage, Mexican style. It's painted with white and green paint.

I'm entering the house and I see an old wooden table, an electric stove, a microwave, and a big old white refrigerator. It's not cute looking. It looks deserted.

At my right side there is a big open space and this is when I find out we are not alone anymore.

Around 12 to 13 people are all over the place, on the floor, everywhere. It's too crowded and hot and smelly.

There is only one old couch and lots of old mattresses on the floor. There is only one fan blowing air for all of us in the room. It's not even enough. I'm sweating already and it's getting difficult to breathe, it is so hot.

I'm hungry, I'm starving. I haven't eaten all day. I don't want to complain. I'm okay. It's alright. Nothing else matters. I'm alive and my sister Jenny, a 25-year-old woman, is still by my side every second that passes.

That night we sleep on the floor on top of the old, ugly looking mattresses. It is very uncomfortable because of the hardness of the surface.

I open my eyes after a long night. I look for my sister. She is right there, drinking a cup of coffee. I smell the coffee in the air. I see the sunshine through the window glass, some people still sleeping.

My stomach is growling, asking for food, letting me know it is empty. I'm hungry.

"Jenny, *tengo hambre*," I say to my sister. She hands me a hard, long Mexican bread and pours black coffee into a plastic cup. The bread is really hard—so hard that when I try to bite on it, it will crumble. So I dip the bread into my coffee and eat it like that.

All my life I've been doing this. I dip whatever I'm eating, cookies or bread, into my juice, milk or soda. It's just something I do all the time. It's just me.

I don't recall eating anything else that day but bread, coffee and lots of tap water.

There is nothing good to watch on TV. All day long all they play is Cantinflas, which is a famous comedy sequel of this poor man with his pants down his ass with suspenders and a little hat.

The TV is very small and it works with an antenna. It is also black and white.

We are told the rules:

- Listen to them.
- Do as they say.
- Stay together, keep the same pace.
- Don't turn back, no buts.

We are divided into three groups. Me and my sister are in the same one.

He is talking to us. He is the coyote, the person in charge of bringing us to the other side of the border. Group #1 is already on its way. They were on the move early in the morning. Each minute that passes is full of tension. The clock keeps ticking and soon it will be my turn.

A couple of hours later, a telephone is ringing. The coyote grabs the telephone. Then he says a code and his nickname. This phone is no ordinary phone. It is black, big, with a long antenna.

The coyote keeps talking on the phone. I'm just so amazed with this object. I've never seen one like that before.

He presses a button and puts it back into his pocket. He says, "Group #1 just arrived at the other side of the border. We have the green light."

It is our turn now.

We all get into a circle, hold hands and pray to the Lady of Guadalupe.

For an instant I feel like she is there, present, watching us, protecting us.

It's getting late and we should be going to sleep. Tomorrow it will be a very long day, and we need to rest. I go to sleep on an empty stomach.

I remember having this dream of being in space, while I'm floating and looking at the rings of Saturn, the gas storms on Jupiter, the Milky Way and the stars. It is just me alone, surrounded by the darkness and the glints of light from the stars that look so much like glitter as I am trying to reach for one.

"*Despiértate*, Esperanza, *levántate.*" Time to wake up. My sister looks ready. I don't know what time it is.

"Everybody, you are just allowed to bring one pair of clothes and one pair of shoes, nothing else." The coyote speaks.

I have to get ready. I brush my teeth. No time for a shower. I'm looking into my luggage, trying to find something to put on as I discover in a corner lots of old backpacks and suitcases with clothes in them. They were left behind by people a long, long time ago, which is the same thing we are about to do. We are leaving our stuff behind. Maybe it'll help somebody else after us.

My sister Jenny is rolling the dollar money and important papers like her ID, phone numbers, and directions to addresses in case of an emergency. She bags it and saves it in her bra, just like mom and grandma used to do when going to the market. As she is doing this, avoiding anyone in the room seeing her, my stomach makes a loud noise. I'm really hungry. I think my sister hears it. She might be hungry as well. I haven't seen her eating. We haven't eaten anything.

She approaches the coyote. She is taking money out of her jeans pocket and handing it to him.

"Can you please get us something to eat? Please."

He says he will as soon as his partner comes back, because he can't leave us in the house by ourselves.

A while later they switch, and then he comes back with two big white shopping bags. There are two two-liter bottles of Jarritos—Mexican soda, pineapple flavor—and inside the bags are tacos—Mexican tacos—he bought from the lady across the street. We have enough tacos to share with everybody. We share them with these poor and worried people and the coyotes. We all ate, I remember. Eating like six tacos by myself, they tasted so delicious.

We asked what they were made of because it didn't look like chicken or steak. The coyote said in a very suspicious way, "You really don't want to know. If I tell, you might stop eating them. All you need to know is that they are made of different parts of pork."

Oh well. It is not really a big deal. It tasted good and I'm not hungry anymore. That's what really matters.

Some time around noon he got a phone call. It's our turn. We've got to be ready, we are going NOW.

After two days of being inside the house with no communication with the outside world, the big wooden door opens and the light is bothering my sight. I step out. The sky is bright blue, sunny with big fluffy white clouds.

I started thinking of my mom, wherever she might be. She is looking at the same sky I'm looking at this exact moment. I feel she is with me, she is watching me. I picture her face in the sky looking down at me.

"I'm getting closer and closer to be with you Mami," I say to myself.

Outside on my left side there is the SUV in the driveway. I don't know if it's the same, but it looks so much like it.

"Get low, stay low, hurry, hurry get in!"

The door is open. I get into the SUV. This time they throw us the black hoods to put them on by ourselves. This has become so familiar to me, I am so used to it, I'm not scared of it anymore.

The doors close. Everyone is inside. I feel the air conditioner on my skin. I can hear the air exiting from the vents. I smell air freshener mixed with body odor all compress inside this packed space.

The car is on the move. I can't see where we are going. All I hear is the motor running.

Sometime later a man says we can take the hoods off our faces. The car keeps moving. I'm confused. He says there is no more need to use them anymore.

The first thing I notice is the big and high steel fence to my right. That's the border. My eyes cannot believe this, so big and close. The street is deserted, no other cars present or people at this time. I keep staring at the wall all the time. The SUV keeps on moving. Some parts of the wall made of steel have graffiti painted on them, plastic flowers and crosses, missing people and wanted posters, and of course, warning signs in both Spanish and English.

The SUV keeps on moving, the driver changing gears, turning the steering wheel, until he stops and meets with a man inside a blue pickup truck. The engine never stops. The man in the pickup waves his hand and the driver keeps on going. Nobody ever got out of the SUV, it was more like everything was well planned, so well organized to avoid any kind of problem.

The SUV stops, no buildings or houses around. I see through the windshield a very deserted area. The prominent color is brown.

The doors get unlocked and they open. We all start to get out. In the air, I smell erosion, dust, rust. The heat is so uncomfortable. I look around. It kind of looks like a junkyard, scrap metal everywhere, cars parted out with just the frame itself.

There is a trailer house with no glass in the windows, no doors. It looks very old and uninhabited.

We are told to follow the coyote inside. While we are on the move a second man is sorting us.

We get inside. It is very dusty and dirty. Picture a big long rectangle, that's what it looks like. It is unfurnished. There is nothing inside.

The coyote hands us black plastic bags like the ones used for construction work, the heavy duty ones.

"Get naked. Everybody now undress!" The coyote has given us an order and we are supposed to follow it.

What does he mean "get naked," is he being for real? Right here, right NOW? His facial expression seems very serious.

He yells again and in a blink of an eye everybody starts to get naked.

I'm trying to focus on myself. I don't want anybody to see me naked. I was told my body is God's sacred tool, and so as I am getting undressed at the same time I am trying to cover myself from others. It isn't an easy task.

I don't remember being curious and trying to see others. I was so concentrated on myself. It was very awkward because we were all strangers with the same dream and situation.

Of course it all happened really fast.

The coyote gives each and every one of us wet suits to put on. They have a very strong smell like rubber. They are black and very difficult to put on. They cover us from our feet all the way to our necks. The zipper is on the back and it has a long string to help us unzip it by ourselves. It is uncomfortable to put it on, trying to fit in and stretch it at the same time. It feels very tight and makes me hotter than before.

Remember the bags we were given. We are to put the clothes we had on inside them, make a knot and double bag them. As I am doing this, the loud sound of a helicopter appears.

"*¡Al suelo, todos al suelo rápido!*" We all get on the floor without thinking of it twice.

Adrenaline starts pumping in my veins. I don't know what's going on. My instinct is to cover my head with my hands. As I'm doing this, I get a flashback from when I was little, living in Nicaragua and being so scared when earthquakes happened. Mami and Daddy would always be present to rescue me, pick me up, and I would feel safe with their arms around me.

The sound stops. The helicopter disappears. We are told everything is fine. We can get back up.

This time Mami and Daddy are not present, just my sister is with me. I say to myself, *I'm okay, you've got this, you can do this*, and somehow courage flows through my body.

The coyote is giving us instructions. Once we exit this trailer, we are told to follow his commands.

We should keep together. No one is to stay behind. If someone does so, we shouldn't go back and play hero. We should keep our bags close to our heads, watch very carefully where we are walking and listen.

The time has come. It's time to leave the trailer and start our quest. Everything seems to be under control.

The sun is bright. This wetsuit is making me sweat so much. It is too hot.

We start walking out, leaving the trailer behind us. We have a man guiding us up front and one behind us, making sure everything goes well.

At my left there is a huge concrete wall and straight ahead all I see is scrap metal, pipes, and these huge square-looking metal frames.

There is no way around it. We can only go through there, avoiding trying to get hurt, being careful. I am ahead, just behind our guide, because I am young, more active and flexible, and I can move faster.

All the time I am on the move, climbing the bars and going under the squares and below. I am always turning back and keeping an eye on my sister. She is pretty far back, and also she is kind of heavy. She manages to do well and never falls behind.

After a while we finally get to the other side and there is an opening in the wall. It isn't very big and it is made in a triangle shape. Nobody is missing. We are all together.

One by one we go through the hole in the wall and get to the other side.

There is water, a pond, a canal, kind of like a river, I can't tell exactly.

No grass, no trees. The hill on the other side of the river is mostly soil. Grass I guess is hard to grow in this unsuitable and brilliant weather.

With my bag in my right hand, and looking around me, I approach the edge of the pond. The coyote is already in.

"Do we have to get into the water?"

"Get in. Hurry up. Get into the water. Jump," he says.

"I don't know how to swim."

"Don't worry. I'm here. It is not deep."

No time to think about it or negotiate. It is out of the question.

I jump into the water. I don't know how it happens. I think I bend my knees, because the water gets into my nostrils. My reflexes quickly kick in. I straighten my legs, get up and cough. There was no way I am going to let this water into my mouth. This water is not clean or treated. The water color is black! Black, can you believe such a thing, how dirty and unhealthy could it be?

"This is bad, this is really bad," I say to myself.

It even smells funky.

I keep spitting because I have this nasty, horrible taste in my mouth. Yuk . . . I think I didn't swallow. I spat and coughed just in time.

We need to walk to the hill, climb it and get to the other side of the metal fence—the border—we can't keep going through the water. It's blocked.

The coyote is the first one on the hill. The next is me. There is a thorny shrub on the way. My suit almost gets caught on it. It scratches my face. I don't notice it at the time until my sister pointed it out.

"What happened to you, Esperanza?" I touched my face and noticed blood on my hand. The salt from my sweat was burning into my scratched face.

Face to face with the famous fence, so high and impenetrable-looking.

At the bottom of the fence there is a hole dug into the ground. Just like the one dogs dig in the backyard.

We get on all fours, and slide through the hole. My hair, my nails, my face are all dirty.

My sister does pretty well. She isn't so huge after all. We laugh, it's so funny! I'm so proud of her. She's keeping up with me. She is doing all this for me.

We jump back into the water. Ahhh, I can't stand the funky smell. It is a combination of motor oil and sulfur.

Time to keep on moving.

Every step I take, I keep on feeling metal objects and pipes on the bottom of my feet. I'm trying to be as careful as I can be because I don't want to trip and fall and repeat the same mistake from before—no, no, no way!

A while later, the coyote shouts, "Slow! Wait! You two go first. Keep your head out and keep the bags close to your heads. Next the three of you. Do the same and follow the current."

What's going on? What's happening? Something is wrong.

Curiosity is killing me, so I turn around and take a look, trying to see around me.

Surprise. I'm in shock.

"OH MY GOD—OH MY GOD! Did he see me? Can he see me? OH MY GOD—OH MY GOD!"

All these questions running in my head. I'm freaking out.

I've seen an officer up on the hill, standing in his brown, greenish uniform with a rifle around his shoulder and binoculars in his left hand.

For some inexplicable reason we didn't get in trouble. The bags were supposed to hide our heads and give the illusion of garbage bags floating on the black and dirty water. Apparently there is no danger anymore.

The coyote tells us to keep moving faster.

What just happened? Impossible! I'm sure he saw me back up there. Why didn't he do anything? We are so lucky! God is on our side.

We keep on walking in this black, dirty stinky water. Ahead of us there is a tunnel. As soon as I start walking into it, I notice plastic crosses, flowers, names written on the walls. The tunnel is kind of dark and I'm getting goose bumps.

"Do people die in here?" I ask myself.

At the other side of the tunnel, at the end, I see far away the end of this water. I can't wait to get there. I'm getting closer and closer . . . to where I really want to be, with my Mommy.

What's that foam on top of the water, white foam with brown stuff on top?

"What is this?"

At my right there's a three to four-foot high hill. It's pretty high. The coyote gives us the order to climb it.

One of the coyotes is up there. The other one is still in the water.

"You go first," he says.

I'm the youngest, the lightest, so I go first. I'm trying and trying to get up there. I'm digging my nails into the ground, digging and digging till I get a grip and try to push myself up. I feel hands holding me. The coyote is helping me and it's being so difficult, I'm feeling so, so heavy. I finally get up the hill . . .

I turn around. Now the only people in the water are my sister, the coyote, and another tall skinny man. They're trying to help my sister to get up. We are running out of time. A lot is going through my mind. These two men are trying to push my sister up the hill. What can I do? I lie down on the ground and start cheering for her, "Vamos, Jenny, tu puedes!" Come on, Jenny come on, you can do it!

I grab her arms and try and try. She is so heavy. Or maybe that was the moment that made it feel so crazily impossible. Between the two guys in the water pushing her up and me, she finally gets up the hill.

"Ahh," I gasp. We are still together.

"Rápido, desnúdense. Cámbiense la ropa." What? Here? Right now? They want us to get naked and get our clothes out of our bags and get dressed? If I did it once, I can do it again. It shouldn't be a problem. My sister is naked already. I'm trying to stay behind this little bush, which doesn't help a lot, because it doesn't even have leaves in it. I open my bag. OH MY GOD!

"What happened?" someone asks me. *My clothes are wet, my clothes are wet.* How did this happen? Now I remember that spiky tree back there when I was crossing the fence.

"You go last," the coyote says. I'm scared, I'm last. We all have to jump this little four-foot wall. On the other side there is a big parking lot and a supermarket, with not a lot of cars around. I'm trying to rinse out my clothes as much as I can.

"*Dios mío, Dios mío, Dios mío,*" I keep saying to myself, just asking for a miracle. My clothes are still wet, but that's not the worst of it, my sneakers are soaked and wet too. I'm in big trouble. They are not stupid—they are leaving me for last, just in case I get in trouble they—the ICE people (immigration)—will take me while all the other ones will be safe. Right now all I'm doing is praying and praying.

Finally after everybody goes into the supermarket it is my turn. Every step I take my shoes go squishy, squishy and leave a trail behind, which evaporates from the hot asphalt. I look behind. I look up front and I see the heat waves. That's how hot it is. All I'm asking is, *Please God, dry my clothes*.

I walk into the supermarket, my shoes squeaking, everyone looking at me. I'm leaving the floor behind me wet. These people are looking at me. I don't know what to do. I don't know what to say. I keep my head up and just act like I'm buying some cookies. This American old couple looks at me like I'm an animal. I will never forget their looks and their heads shaking in disapproval.

One by one, two by two, we will start getting into a truck outside waiting for us. Again I'm the last one. Am I going to get in trouble at some point? I'm just waiting. It can happen, I know it is possible.

There is a gray pickup with a camper in the back where soon we will get in. We all are stacked, yeah, one on top of the other one. It is so hot. We're all sweating. We're all stinking, and on top of us they throw a heavy blanket.

OH MY GOD. It's getting worse. I'm about to get a heat stroke. I'm just trying to keep my breathing in sync.

"*Concéntrate,* Esperanza. *Concéntrate.*" My sister is in the front passenger seat, while I'm burning from inside out. The pickup keeps on moving. I can't wait to get to wherever they are bringing us. My breathing becomes slower, and slower . . .

OVERCOMING THE MARKS THAT REMAIN . . .

"How Do You See Me?"

Anjelique Wadlington

 Anjelique began writing in 2004 with Herstory's very first work-shop in Riverhead Correctional Facility, so that her journey to give voice to incarcerated women begins with our own. From that moment on, she has never stopped writing. Nor has she stopped working to help others through her words, so that even when she was sent upstate to complete her sentence she stayed in close touch. In 2008 when she was released she became part of our first group of speakers, reading to students of criminology, sociology and law all over Long Island, and took part in the organization of a "bridges" workshop to allow women coming out of jail to write with women from the larger community.

The story that we have reproduced here was commissioned in 2010 by the Women on the Job Project of the Women's Fund of Long Island, to illuminate what happens when women with felony convictions seek employment, and has been read by various task forces working on Second Chance legislation which would allow for the expunging of certain criminal records and have remained successful in reentry for a five-year period following their release. It was a high-light of a conference hosted by the Suffolk County Reentry Task Force on "Cre-ating Positive Solutions to the Barriers of Reentry: A Family Affair."

In 2013, Anjie became one of the primary speakers for a Raise the Age New York press conference bringing together government officials, clergy, and community organizations from all over Long Island. She is pictured here addressing reporters during the historic hour when DA Kathleen Rice became the first district attorney to lend public support to efforts to raise the age of criminal responsibility in New York State.

While working full-time, she attends Suffolk County Community College, through a scholarship that will cover her expenses through graduate school, wherever she decides to study next, allowing her to work toward her dream of becoming a social worker.

I did my last check in my rearview mirror, my make up was perfect. Nice and simple, I had left it natural with a light lipgloss. My hair was straightened with a little flip in the front. I wanted to make a great impression. Mommy had always told me, "Your first impression is the only and most important impression you can make." So I always made sure of it. The sun was shining bright and at its peak, so I knew everything was going to go without a hitch.

Change wasn't anything I was fond of; I hate having to jump into things or rearranging my daily schedule. I was perfectly fine until I noticed I had to get out of my car and hit the alarm. I wasn't in my skin, because I had to enter another. I felt grown and professional when I dressed up. Like the people do in the City. They looked important, which made me feel important, *I want a cigarette, I need to calm my nerves, I just don't want to smell like I just came from a bar, walking into the building.* The building wasn't too far from where I had parked, so I just had to tough it out.

I decided to wear black slacks creased to perfection by my own hands. Like I had learned when I wore my uniforms. It's been a few years since then. I haven't really needed to use an iron recently, but some skills you never forget. I had decided to go with a nice simple button-down blouse with a bright tank top underneath. "Never show any of your secret body parts, you don't want to portray something you aren't," Mommy had said to me over the phone as I got dressed earlier.

It seemed to be a longer walk than I thought it would be, or my feet were just dragging and digging into the concrete. *What will they ask? Will they like me? Or am I just like everyone else? Will I get a chance to explain my answer?*

I don't know really know what to expect. I just hope they give me the chance. Picking my head high and hands to my side, I knew I was out of place. *What am I doing here?* Another thought crossed my mind, as I seemed to walk slower.

I felt the slacks hit my legs in each step I took—one was green and one black. My shoes decided to feel flat. I was no longer wearing my heels. My feet started to hurt. My boots were tight, hot, and sweaty. My shirt seemed to get tighter at the neck, as the bowtie got more uncomfortable.

I gave myself a quick glance down to see that I was no longer in my semi suit, but I was in full uniform of forest green and white. My pants were no longer black. They had become inmate green. I felt the goose bumps run across my arms and a feeling of embarrassment as everyone pointed and laughed. The number read across my shirt 05g0418. I realized that I had jumped out of my professional skin into a skin I didn't want to be in anymore, but lived with for years and recognized well, one that I had left years ago to die.

I walked to the building. *Ready Anj? Take a deep breath,* I told myself getting closer and closer to the office building. I placed my hand on the door and jumped into my white girl skin, just still black. It had worked a lot over the years when I had to speak to clients over the phone or complaining customers when I used to work at Bagel Boss. I entered the quiet fully carpeted office.

"Hello, may I help you?" a tall man had asked.

"Yes, my name is Anjelique. I am here to speak with Joe Lepton," as I extended my right hand out to shake his pale cold hand. My dad used to tell me you can tell a lot in a person by their handshake. If it was firm, weak. It gives them character without having to say a word.

"Yes, that's me," as he firmly shook my hand back. *Strong willed,* I thought to myself.

"I had called you yesterday morning for the job that the company had listed on the internet," I said as I looked him in his eyes.

"Yes, it is nice to meet you. Come, come in."

He seemed to be uneasy after I had told him that I was the woman who had called him. The dumb found look on his face, as I have seen many times over the years. When the voice doesn't match the other person's body, or color.

We walked to a smaller office around the corner where it looked like they have their business meetings. It's real, a REAL office, where real things are discussed. I was so amazed to actually be invited in. He directed me to sit across from him.

"So did you fill out the application?" he asked.

"No, Sir, I haven't."

"Okay," as he shuffled in the bottom draw of the desk we sat at. He pulled out a book . . . well, it seemed to be. I looked wide-eyed and shook my head before he started to raise his body up. "Okay, fill this out and we will talk after you are done," he directed me.

"Yes." I had responded back with a light smile. He got up and excused himself and headed toward the office door.

"Do you have a pen?" he asked trying to test my preparation skills.

One thing I had learned on my own throughout the years. Always be prepared for the unknown. You never know when you need a pen and paper. I nodded yes. And he exited the office and closed the door lightly.

Breezing through the first few basic knowledge questions of myself and morality questions I had stumbled and ignored one. If I didn't know, I skipped. Finish the rest and go back to it later on towards the end of the test. I hear all my exam teachers' voices over the years of test taking. Maybe I just didn't want to face these questions. Or maybe I didn't want them to know my weakness and what I feared.

Have you ever been convicted of a felony? If yes, for what and when?

The question was there. In plain sight! It wasn't going to go anywhere. I went around the question. I tried to even act like it didn't even exist. I really just wanted to get up and walk out. Maybe even lie. How will they find out? I thought I had dealt with it, but I was not ready to face it. Yes . . .

I just stared at the completed application. Incomplete thoughts and "what if's" and "I just hope so." Until a light knock on the door and his head popped in.

"Everything okay?" he asked cheerfully.

"Yes," and I turned my head looking back and smiled.

He came in and sat back into his chair and looked over the application. He nodded his head as if he was impressed. I just made sure I always looked at him and smiled.

"Okay. I have two questions. First, why should I hire you?"

I really wanted to say, *Because I need a job. And I am broke and I am parole mandated.* But I didn't, I couldn't sound desperate. So I was logical about it. And he just nodded and smiled while I answered his question.

"Good, I like that. Question Two, I see you checked yes for being convicted of a felony and that you will explain in interview. Well, here is your chance." And he sat there and made it so easy.

"I was young . . . 17; I sold drugs to an undercover for my boyfriend. He told to save his own ass, but I had refused to talk or to have knowledge of anyone else in the drug game." He just actually sat there and listened, the last stranger to ever listen to me was no one.

"I learned my lesson, but that doesn't define who I am. And what I can be. I am a very loyal and dependable person. I complete what I start," I commented before he spoke.

"I will hire you, I think this is a great opportunity for you, and you will be a huge asset to this company. Call me on Monday for your schedule so we can set you up with a patient," he said extending his hand to shake mine.

I was part of something! The cocoons hatched and the wings spread wide. They were beautiful and ready to continue their journey. I wanted to scream for joy and excitement, but it had to wait.

"Thank you, thank you so much," as I shook his hand back and exited the small office, around the corner to the door, to exit my past and enter a promising future doing what I loved.

The weekend seemed to not matter. I was working Monday, and nothing made me change my mood, or steal my shine.

Monday came and I was up at 6 A.M. I got myself together and waited until the office opened at 8. "Good morning, Senior Care. How may I direct your call?" the receptionist had answered on the other end.

"Yes I would like to speak to Joe Lepton. My name is Anjelique Wadlington."

"Hold, please." The music came on to keep me entertained.

"Anjelique, Hi how are you?" Joe had answered on the line.

"I am doing well, and yourself?" being polite.

"Well, thank you. I looked over your application and I spoke to my brother who is my partner. And I am sorry, but it isn't going to work out," he informed me. I just stood in my bedroom in silence. I was heartbroken. And the tears flooded my eyes.

"Okay. Thank you. Have a good day." And I hung up quickly. I felt my final sentencing. The judge has spoken once again, and my fate was in his hand . . .

.

CALL TO ACTION

Where Activists and Storytellers Come Together

Now that you have finished reading these stories, before their impact leaves you, we urge you to think about how you might use this book to take action and to engage others. Will you take the power that comes from each young person's newly discovered truth to spur your own action? Will you bring youth justice reform into places that mere rhetoric cannot go?

Many of us have never visited a prison, yet almost all of us know someone who was incarcerated or affected by impact of incarceration. What this book and the larger social justice movement demands of us, is to take action.

Where activists and storytellers come together, therein lies the heart of hope and true change. The ability to affect policies and minds about young people impacted by the system often comes with the telling of a story, and in hearing each compelling story we ask, "What can we do to make change?" What our lawmakers and communities must hear is our voices, voices raised to tell the jolting experiences of young people in prisons and jails.

A memory so vivid it remains in the forefront of my mind is that of the large, brown eyes of a young women whom I stooped down to peer in at through the tiny opening, just large enough to slide a food tray through, of her prison cell. She was very young and I was visiting a New York State women's prison. I don't remember her name, but I will never forget her eyes, haunting me, seeming to tell me their story of her final acceptance of imprisonment and defeat of the soul.

It is this memory that I carry with me when I talk to our growing audiences about our hopes and dreams for a more responsive and ever expanding coalition of community members. No longer can we accept our failure as a community to acknowledge the very real and devastating effect locking children up takes on us and our future generation. No longer can we punish the spirit of children by subjecting them to a failed system.

Let us pledge to share these stories of our youth's struggle to survive, with our families, friends, and colleagues, using them in our schools and taking them to advocate for change with our lawmakers. Let us create reading circles, meet with legislators, and encourage community dialogue, all in an effort to reform how the system treats young people. Let us take up the torch, refusing to sit silently as our children continue to be victimized by the very system put in place to protect them. If you want to take action and are not sure where to begin, contact Herstory Writers Workshop at (631) 676-7395/ or sliguori@herstorywriters.org. You can also contact Angelo Pinto, Campaign Manager of the Correctional Association of New York's Raise the Age campaign at (212) 254-5700, ext. 325/ or apinto@correctionalassociation.org.

The Correctional Association and Herstory are available to present at your organization, church, program or school. We can send you relevant information, let you know what the campaign is up to, and help you find ways to add the power of your own voice to the voices found on these pages to the call to action found within the heart of these stories.

We hope you will take a look at the new next few pages which hold a wealth of resources to guide you as you journey to create a better system, one more fair and responsible to the needs of our young people.

Onward,

Serena Liguori
Herstory Writers Workshop
Advocacy and Justice Program Director

TAKING BACK OUR CHILDREN

It's Time to Take Back Our Children

Each year, nearly 50,000 16- and 17-year-olds are arrested as adults in New York State.[1] Because they are defined by the law as adults, these youth can be questioned by police without parental notification and confined in adult prisons and jails. They also do not have access to the effective and developmentally appropriate rehabilitative services that are available in Family Court.[2]

Young people housed in adult prisons and jails are in grave danger. Children in adult prisons and jails face very high rates of sexual assault and rape,[3] physical assaults,[4] and attacks with weapons,[5] and they can be held in solitary confinement for long periods of time.[6] Children in adult jails are also far more likely to commit suicide than children in youth detention facilities.[7]

Research demonstrates that prosecuting and sentencing children as adults not only presents threats to children's safety and well-being, but also decreases public safety. A strong body of evidence shows that young people charged as adults are more likely to commit violence and crime in the future as compared to young people prosecuted in the youth justice system.[8]

Youth who are convicted as adults may have to carry that mark with them for the rest of their lives, making it difficult for them to get on the right path and become productive and healthy adults. The aftermath of a lifelong criminal record can include significant barriers to college admission and employment; potential deportation; and the loss of housing for both themselves and their families.[9] This has a negative impact on both young people and our nation's economy.

This issue impacts some communities much harder than others. Because they are more likely to be targeted by the police[10] and are disproportionately represented at virtually every point in the justice system,[11] young people of color are more likely than white children to bear the serious and lasting consequences of being charged and incarcerated as adults.[12]

Why Raise the Age?

All children have a right to safety and to access developmentally appropriate services, programs, education, and treatment. Compared to those who have been prosecuted in the youth justice system, young people who have been charged as adults have been shown to be more likely to recidivate and return to prison.[13] Moreover, adult prisons and jails are not properly equipped to provide safety or services to children.[14]

Over the last decade, many states, including nearby Connecticut, have successfully raised the age of criminal responsibility without overwhelming the courts or the youth justice system. In 2011, after adjusting for inflation, Connecticut spent $2 million less on its youth justice system than it had ten years earlier despite (or because of) having raised the age and increased spending on community services.[15] After raising the age, Connecticut also saw total arrests and violent crime arrests plummet.[16] Usually a leader in criminal justice reform, New York State is shamefully behind on this issue. This outdated law puts our children, our economy and public safety at risk.

How Should the Age Be Raised?

- The age of criminal responsibility should be raised for all young people, regardless of the offense they are charged with
- No one under the age of 18 should ever be confined in an adult jail or prison

What Would Raising the Age Do?

- Increase public safety
- Limit dangers to youth
- Provide healthier avenues for our young people to change, grow and develop

- Increase the number of young people eligible for education and employment opportunities

Harsh Realities

- New York is one of only two states in the country that prosecutes all 16- to 17-year-olds charged with a crime in the adult criminal justice system, regardless of the severity of their alleged crime. New York also treats 13-, 14-, and 15-year-olds accused of committing certain serious crimes as "juvenile offenders" (J.O.s), prosecuting these young people as adults unless their cases are transferred to Family Court.
- In NYS, 16- and 17-year-olds detained or incarcerated via a criminal court order are confined in adult prisons and jails (youth convicted of juvenile offenses are confined in youth facilities until at least 16, at which time they can be transferred to adult prisons).
- 16- and 17-year-olds in New York State Department of Corrections and Community Supervision (DOCCS) prisons are housed side-by-side with adults. There are no separate residential areas for these young people and they often share large dormitory-style rooms with multiple adults.
- Children in adult jails are 36 times more likely to commit suicide than those in youth detention facilities.[17]
- Children in adult facilities are nearly fifty percent more likely to face an armed attack while inside, and nearly 100% as likely to be beaten by staff as compared to young people in youth facilities.[18]
- The National Prison Rape Elimination Commission found that ¡more than any other group of incarcerated persons, youth incarcerated with adults are probably at the highest risk for sexual abuse.[19]
- Nationwide, youth in adult prisons and jails can be placed in solitary confinement, for days, weeks, months and even years.[20]
- Children in solitary confinement in New York State are fed through a slot in their cell door; do not leave their cells to attend school, programs, or activities; and are allowed only one hour of "recreation" alone in an empty outdoor pen. They are not allowed to make phone calls, including to their parents or other family members.[21]

- There were 560 placements of young people aged 18 and under in the Special Housing Unit (SHU) in the New York State prison system in 2011.[22]
- Extended isolation can be psychologically shattering for anyone, but it is especially harmful for developing adolescent minds.[23]
- A study of New York and New Jersey youth charged with felonies where in New York the youth were prosecuted as adults and in NJ the youth were prosecuted in juvenile court, found that New York youth were 100% more likely to be rearrested for a violent offense and 47% more likely to be rearrested for a property offense. The New York youth were also more frequently rearrested for such offenses and had a 26% greater chance of being reincarcerated.[24]
- Nationwide, youth who are transferred or "waived" into the adult court system are 34% more likely to commit violent or general crime than youth prosecuted in juvenile courts.[25]

Get involved

INVITE the Correctional Association's campaign organizers to present at your organization, church, program or school. Contact our *Raise the Age* Campaign Manager Angelo Pinto at

apinto@correctionalassociation.org

or (212) 254-5700.

VISIT us online at

http://www.correctionalassociation.org/campaigns/raise-the-age

Notes

1. Department of Criminal Justice Services, *Criminal Justice Case Processing of 16–17 Year Olds* (2010 data), on file with the author (in 2010, there were 45,692 arrests of 16- and 17-year-olds in New York State); Governor's Children's Cabinet Advisory Board, *Advancing a Fair and Just Age of Criminal Responsibility for Youth in New York State* (January 2011) (in 2009, there were 47,339 16- and 17-year-olds in New York State).
2. See generally Judge Michael A. Corriero, Judging Children as Children: Reclaiming New York's Progressive Tradition 56 *N.Y.L. Sch. L. Rev.* 1413 (2011–12) (discussing the options available to family court judges that are not available to adult criminal or supreme court judges).
3. Alan Beck, Marcus Berzofsky, Rachel Caspar, and Christoper Krebs, Depart-

ment of Justice, Bureau of Justice Statistics, *Sexual Victimization in Prisons and Jails Reported by Inmates, National Inmate Survey 2011–12* (May 2013), *http://www.bjs.gov/content/pub/pdf/svpjri1112.pdf;* Alan Beck, Paige, Harrison, Devon Adams, U.S. Department of Justice, Office of Justice Programs, Bureau of Justice Statistics, *Sexual Violence Reported by Correctional Authorities, 2006* (August 2007), *http://www.bjs.gov/content/pub/pdf/svrca06. pdf;* and Alan Beck and Paige Harrison, U.S. Department of Justice, Office of Justice Programs, Bureau of Justice Statistics, *Sexual Violence Reported by Correctional Authorities, 2005* (July 2006), *http://www.bjs.gov/index.cfm?ty= pbdetail&iid=1152.*

4. Martin Forst, Jeffrey Fagan and T. Scott Vivona, "Youth in Prisons and Training Schools: Perceptions and Consequences of the Treatment–Custody Dichotomy," *Juvenile and Family Court Journal,* 40 (1) (1989).

5. Forst, Fagan, and Vivona, "Youth in Prisons and Training Schools."

6. *Growing Up Locked Down: Youth in Solitary Confinement in Jails and Prisons Across the United States* (October 2012), *http://www.aclu.org/criminal-law-reform/growing-locked-down-youth-solitary-confinement-jails-and-prisons-across-united.*

7. Arya Neelum, *Jailing Juveniles: The Dangers of Incarcerating Youth in Adult Jails in America* 1 (2007), *Campaign for Youth Justice, http://www.campaignfor youthjustice.org/documents/CFYJNR_JailingJuveniles.pdf.*

8. Angela McGowan et al., "Effects on Violence of Laws and Policies Facilitating the Transfer of Juveniles from the Juvenile Justice System to the Adult Justice System: A Systematic Review," Department of Health and Human Services, Centers for Disease Control and Prevention, *Morbidity and Mortality Weekly Report,* November 30, 2007, Vol. 56, No. RR-9. (The independent, nonfederal Task Force on Community Preventive Services conducted a review of published scientific evidence concerning the effectiveness of laws and policies that facilitate the transfer of juveniles to the adult criminal justice system. The review and resulting report found that transfer to the adult criminal justice system typically increases rather than decreases rates of violence among transferred youth and recommends against laws or policies facilitating the transfer of juveniles to the adult criminal justice system for the purpose of reducing violence.) Richard E. Redding, "Juvenile Transfer Laws: An Effective Deterrent to Delinquency?" *Juvenile Justice Bulletin* (U.S. Department of Justice Office of Juvenile Justice and Delinquency Prevention) (June 2010), *https://www.ncjrs.gov/pdffiles1/ ojjdp/220595.pdf.*

9. Corriero, *Judging Children as Children.*

10. Neelum Arya and Ian Augarten, *Critical Condition: African-American Youth in the Justice System, Campaign for Youth Justice* (September 2008), *http://www. campaignforyouthjustice.org/documents/CFYJPB_CriticalCondition_000.pdf* (addressing the disproportional treatment of African-American youth in the justice system); *Stop-and-Frisk Campaign: About the Issue,* New York Civil Liberties Union (NYCLU), *www.nyclu.org/issues/racial-justice/stop-and-frisk-practices* (the NYCLU data is specific to New York City).

11. James Bell and Laura John Ridolfi, The W. Haywood Burns Institute, *Adoration of the Question: Reflections on the Failure to Reduce Racial & Ethnic Disparities in the Juvenile Justice System* (Shadi Rahimi ed., 2008), *http://sc-county01.co.santa-cruz.ca.us/prb/jdai/bi_dmc.pdf;* The National Council on

Crime and Delinquency, *And Justice for Some, Differential Treatment of Youth of Color in the Justice System* (2007), *http://www.nccdglobal.org/sites/default/files/publication_pdf/justice-for-some.pdf*.

12. The National Council on Crime and Delinquency, *And Justice for Some*.

13. Richard Redding, "Juvenile Transfer Laws"; McGowan et al., *Effects on Violence of Laws and Policies*.

14. Patricia Allard & Malcolm Young, Prosecuting Juveniles in Adult Court: Perspectives for Policymakers and Practitioners, *J. of Forensic Psychol. Prac.* 65 (2002); Nellis, *Addressing the Collateral Consequences for Young Offenders*.

15. Justice Policy Institute, *Juvenile Justice Reform in Connecticut: How Collaboration and Commitment Improved Outcomes for Youth* (October 2012), *http://towfoundation.org/wp-content/uploads/2013/03/JPI_shortreport_web.pdf*.

16. Justice Policy Institute, *Juvenile Justice Reform in Connecticut*.

17. Arya, *Jailing Juveniles*.

18. Forst, Fagan, Vivona, "Youth in Prisons and Training Schools."

19. *National Prison Rape Elimination Commission Report* (June 2009), at 18, *http://www.ncjrs.gov/pdffiles1/226680.pdf*.

20. Amy Fettig, Teenagers Too Often Wind Up in Solitary, *The New York Times* (June 5 2012), *http://www.nytimes.com/roomfordebate/2012/06/05/when-to-punish-a-young-offender-and-when-to-rehabilitate/the-dangers-of-juveniles-in-solitary-confinement*.

21. New York Civil Liberties Union, *Boxed In: The True Cost of Extreme Isolation in New York's Prisons* (2012), *http://www.nyclu.org/files/publications/nyclu_boxedin_FINAL.pdf*.

22. NYS Department of Correctional Services Locator System, *Summary of New Placements into SHU Cells, Offenders Aged 18 and Under Only, during 01/01/11–12/31/11*, available at *http://www.boxedinny.org/library/* (click on "Prisoner Population in Special Housing Units," and then "Prisoners Newly Placed into SHU Cells Aged 18 and Younger 2007–2011") (note that this document reflects unique placements, and that the same individual may have multiple placements within an annual period).

23. *Growing Up Locked Down*.

24. Redding, "Juvenile Transfer Laws" citing Jeffrey Fagan, Aaron Kupchick and Akiva Liberman, *Be Careful What You Wish For: The ComparativeImpacts of Juvenile versus Criminal Court Sanctions on Recidivism among Adolescent Felony Offenders*.

25. McGowan et al, *Effects on Violence of Laws and Policies*.

Acknowledgements

HERSTORY WRITERS WORKSHOP

This volume would not have come into being without the collective effort of the 200-plus women and adolescent girls who pass through Herstory Writers Workshop's weekly writing circles in Long Island's three jails ever year. The choice that each young woman represented made, for her work to become public in the interest of serving those who will follow, is very moving to see.

We are deeply grateful to the facilitators who have worked with the adolescents represented in this volume, Linda Coleman, Lynn Doris, Silvia Heredia, and Lonnie Mathis, for bringing out each story that appears in these pages.

We are grateful to Linda Coleman and Erika Duncan for editing this collection, which appeared as its own section of Herstory's larger anthology *VOICES: Memoirs from Long Island's Correctional Facilities,* published in 2012, to Herstory's advocacy and justice program director, Serena Liguori for helping us to connect each piece to the issues it touches, and to Gabrielle Horowitz-Prisco, the director of the Juvenile Justice Project of the Correctional Association of New York for becoming a second reader for our introductory remarks.

We thank Angelo Pinto of the Raise the Age Campaign of the Juvenile Justice Project of the Correctional Association of New York for the energy and imagination he has brought to the creation of this special edition to be used in the campaign. We thank our colleagues and partners in this effort at Hofstra University, Stony Brook University, St. John's University, Adelphi University, SUNY College at Old Westbury, St. Joseph's College, Queensborough Community College, Suffolk Community College, Farmingdale State College and CW Post, and the organizations that have come together to bring players from Long Island into the Juvenile Justice Reform Campaign, Prison Families, Anonymous, Family Support Long Island at Molloy College, the Unitarian Universalist Congregation at Shelter Rock, and the Suffolk and Nassau County Chapters of New York Civil Liberties Union.

None of this would be possible without the ongoing support and good will of the now retired corrections officers, Lieutenant Darlene McClurkin and Sergeant Noreen Fisher at Riverhead Correctional Facility, Captain Helen Geslak and Jonathan Scherr, program director of the DWI Facility at Yaphank. We thank the officers who have lovingly selected and supported the teen writers in Nassau County Correctional Facility.

As the project took shape, its funders provided us with much more than money. We thank the Women's Fund of Long Island for the first seed money that allowed us to start to work in Riverhead Jail, the Long Island Unitarian Universalist Fund (in Long Island Community Foundation), the Chase and Stephanie Coleman Foundation, and the Office of Suffolk County Legislator Vivian-Viloria Fisher for the funding that allowed us to sustain our project and bring it to Yaphank Correctional Facility as well. We thank Eastern Suffolk BOCES for seeing to potential of our project to further educational goals, and for lending the support that helps us to bring our work to younger women writing in Suffolk County's jails year after year, as well.

We thank the Ms Foundation for Women and Ben & Jerry's Foundation for funding our first *Youth Writing for Justice* Programs, allowing us to expand our work with adolescents incarcerated into Nassau County, while beginning to work on this volume and engage college activists in interacting with the stories produced. We thank Long Island Unitarian Universalist Fund for supporting our taking this work into the advocacy arena, Amy Hagedorn and the Long Island Community Foundation for direct support of Herstory's work with the "Raise the Age Work, and Francine and Philip Medaglia for supporting a special reprinting of *VOICES.*"

The conceptual work underlying this work would never have been possible without the continued friendship, active guidance and loving friendship of Angela Zimmerman and Deborah Barrett-Anderson during their tenure at the Nassau County Youth Board. We thank our board of directors for helping us to chart our direction as we moved from a writing project empowering individual women into the larger use of our "dare to care" pedagogy to change hearts, minds and policies, and most especially the late, Roslyn Muraskin, pioneer in feminist criminology who brought our work to the attention of an international audience through including us in *It's a Crime/Women and Justice,* the text that she edited over the years.

We thank Natalie Byfield, professor of sociology at St. John's University and visiting research scholar with John Jay College of Criminal Justice, for her examination of these stories and the changes in the lives of the women who wrote them as she posited a new way of looking at restoration and guilt in victimless crimes. We thank Suzy Dalton Sonenberg, Herstory's development director for the larger perspective and dreams she has brought to this project.

We thank Jim Harris of G&H SOHO, Inc. (*www.ghsoho.com*) for his personal involvement and caring work with us as the printer of this volume.

We thank the young people, both incarcerated and free who have written their stories with the hope that their words might play a part in creating a more just, equitable world.

It is our dream that this small folio volume will eventually be underwritten to the extent that it will be able to be given away free of charge, wherever there are young people fighting for justice where a story might help pave the way.

Acknowledgements

THE CORRECTIONAL ASSOCIATION OF NEW YORK

This effort would not have been possible without the vision, energy and creativity of the Herstory Writer's Workshop, and the courage and resilience of the teenage girls and young women whose stories grace these pages. The willingness of these writers to put pen to paper and speak their truths inspires us, and their ability to harness pain into a force for change moves us. Erika Duncan and Serena Liguori of Herstory: you could not be more supportive or effective collaborators. Thank you.

We also thank the members of the Take Back Our Children Alliance, a network of organizations, advocates, families and youth that support long-overdue comprehensive youth justice reform in New York State. We are proud to work alongside all of you. Together we are more than the sum of our parts.

We are deeply grateful to the Tow Foundation, the Public Welfare Foundation and the Horace and Amy Hagedorn Fund. You make our work possible.

We are grateful also to the wonderful Board of Directors and staff of the Correctional Association of New York. We are fortunate to be guided and supported by such able colleagues. Caitlin Kundrat: you are creative and diligent in equal measure, and your work on this project was immeasurably helpful. Many thanks.

Finally, we would like to acknowledge the children, families and communities who are impacted by legislation and policies allowing children to be prosecuted as adults and incarcerated in adult jails and prisons. You are the reason we do this work.

It is our sincere hope that this book will make clear the tragic failures of New York State's laws regarding children in the justice system, and also illuminate new possibilities. We hope that the stories you have just read will help change the lives of many of New York State's children and families, and help us create stronger and safer communities. The reality is that the real way to help public safety is also the right way to help children. It is time to translate that knowledge into law.

Call to Action: Notes

Call to Action: Notes